# The Mysteries of the Goths

# The Mysteries of the Goths

Edred

Limited First Edition

© Rûna-Raven Press, 2007

All rights reserved. No part of this book, either in part or in whole, may be reproduced, transmitted or utilized in any form or by any means electronic, photographic or mechanical, including photo-copying, recording, or by any information storage and retrieval system, without the permission in writing from the Publisher, except for brief quotations embodied in literary articles and reviews.

For permissions, or for the serialization, condensation, or for adaptation write the Publisher at the address below.

Printed in the USA

ISBN: 1-885972-31-8

Rûna-Raven Press
P. O. Box 557
Smithville, Texas 78957
USA

www.runaraven.com

This limited first edition of *The Mysteries of the Goths* is bound in purple with silver ink and is limited to 500 copies, of which this is number.

# Abbreviations

ch.   chapter
OHG   Old High German
OS    Old Saxon
Go.   Gothic
Lat.  Latin
OE    Old English
ON    Old Norse
PGmc. Proto-Germanic
PIE   Proto-Indo-European
pl.   plural
sg.   singular

## Note on Phonetic Representations

Spellings which appear in square brackets indicate the approximate phonetic sound of a word, as opposed to its usual spelling in any given language.

# Acknowledgments

The author would like to acknowledge the editorial help provided on certain sections of this book by Alice Rhoades, Yasha Hartberg and Michael Starks.

Special notes of gratitude also go to Betty Eden Flowers for her work on the numerical index of the Gothic vocabulary and to Ian Read for his research expedition to Horace Walpole's Gothic mansion, Strawberry Hill.

Notes of thanks also go to Michael Moynihan and James Chisholm.

# Table of Contents

Preface............................................................................................9
Introduction...................................................................................11
Chapter One: Out of the Womb of Nations...........................15
   Historical Frameworks........................................................ 15
      Origins of the Goths....................................................15
      The Name "Goth"........................................................ 17
      Early Migrations...........................................................19
      The Hunnic Revolution............................................... 20
      The Ostrogoths.............................................................21
      The Visigoths...............................................................23
      The Gothic Legacy..................................................... 25
   History of the Gothic Tradition: Exoteric and Esoteric........29
      Exoteric..........................................................................29
      Esoteric........................................................................ 29

Chapter Two: The Mysteries of the Gothic Church..................35
   The Ancient Gothic Religion...........................................35
      The Spiritual World....................................................36
         Soul Conceptions................................................... 36
         Funerary Customs................................................. 38
         Spirits and Demons............................................... 41
         Ancestral Spirits................................................... 42
         Gods and Goddesses............................................ 43
            Individual Gods............................................ 44
               Gauts...................................................... 44
               *Teiws.....................................................45
               *Fairguneis..............................................46
               *Iggws....................................................46
      Cosmology....................................................................47
      Cultic Forms............................................................... 48
         Timing......................................................................48
         Priests......................................................................49
         Pagan Ritual Elements......................................... 51
            Sacrifice........................................................ 51
            Shrines.......................................................... 55
            Holy Objects............................................... 55
               Spears......................................................55
               Rings....................................................... 56
               Kettles..................................................... 56
         Magic and Divination............................................ 57
            Magic.............................................................57
            Divination......................................................58
         Myths and Legends................................................58

Gothic Christianity..................................................................60
   Christianization of the Goths..................................60
   Tenets of the Gothic Church.................................... 62
   Ritual of the Gothic Church..................................... 62
      Gothic Ritual................................................... 64
      Ancient Gothic Church Structures........................ 65
      The Gothic Bible.............................................. 66

Chapter Three: Mysteries of the Gothic Alphabet
    and the Gothic Cabbala..............................................69
   The Gothic Alphabet.....................................................72
   The Esoteric Meanings of the Gothic Letters....................76
   The Gothic Cabala...................................................... 82
      Numerology........................................................82
   Gothic Gamatria........................................................ 86

Chapter Four: The Hidden Treasures of the Goths...................89
   The Treasure of Pietroassa............................................89
   The Visigothic Treasure of Alaric...................................92
   The Treasure of Fuente de Guarrazar........................... 95
   The Visigothic Treasure-Tower of Secrets....................... 98

Chapter Five: Spears of Destiny............................................101
   Ancient Gothic Spears................................................101
   The "Holy Lance"......................................................105

Chapter Six: Notes toward the Esoteric Gothic Legacy............ 109
   The Cagots..............................................................109
   The Visigoths and the Mystery of Rennes-le-Château..........112

Appendix A: The Pronunciation of the Gothic Language.......... 115
Appendix B: History of the Word "Gothic"
   and its Connotations................................................... 119
Appendix C: The Spiritual Heritage of the Goths
   By Bishop **X**, GCG................................................... 123
Appendix D The Gothic Mission Today................................ 127

Select Bibliography............................................................. 129

# Preface

This book has had a mysterious fate. It was conceived in the summer of 1977, when I formally studied the Gothic language at the university, it was further developed in the 1980s as new material was gathered on my researches in Europe and finally outlined in the early 1990s. By the dawn of the new millennium, I felt I could bequeath this valuable and precious project to a trusted student and colleague to complete. This idea proved to be misguided on my part, as the student proved untrustworthy and unable to fulfill the vision of the book. The project was soon back on my schedule of works to complete.

Most would-be "magical" explorers of the "inner mysteries of the Goths" simply reduce what they do not already understand to what they already know. The method used for this book requires objective analysis followed up by a form of insight that takes the diverse aspects into account. One can not say, for example, that the Gothic letters are "really" runes and treat them as such. The Gothic letters and mysteries which envelop them are a distinct result of the great cultural synthesis achieved by the Goths in southern Europe. To reduce this achievement to just another example of well-known universal template of "understanding" is a mistake which causes the observer to miss that which is essential. It is a rather odd and ironic trait of the "eclectic mind" that it really desires nothing more than to reduce all the diverse and vibrant forms of the human spirit, to homogenize them, into one universal (and easily grasped) paradigm.

The Goths are a people now lost in the mists of time. Unraveling the mysteries which surround them is a significant challenge, and not one that can be taken lightly. This is not a work of strict scholarship; however, the methods and bases of data used by scholars have been used as the *foundation* of this work. The present book is the result of a subjection of scholarly data to certain spiritual insights which revivify the data as authentic foundations of inner work. In some ways this book is an introduction to more extensive possible works by others who have been initiated into these radical methods. In order to undertake such work, one must first master the objective data — history, languages, cultural studies (including religious and mythological paradigms) — then subject these data to deep contemplation. They must be internalized in order to become the foundations for insight. Once this insight is gained the student is transformed and the student has no choice but to act in the world as a master.

Edred
Woodharrow
May 5, 2007

# Introduction

In the annals of great mysteries, in the annals of mythic greatness, there is no people in the history of Europe of greater mystery combined with tragic greatness than the Goths. They are a folk shrouded in a dark mystique linked to a noble past. Their name has continued to evoke mystery and greatness centuries after they disappeared from political history. This book is intended to explore the Gothic mysteries— of which there are many — and bring to their mist-filled world the light of illumination. In the end we will discover that the Goths were themselves a people of light surrounded by darkness— a darkness which eventually enveloped them. Luckily a great deal of literature already exists on the history of the Goths in English. However, this literature is generally only of the most mundane sort, e.g. political histories. This material forms an indispensable foundation for further studies, but the present book seeks to go beyond these limits into matters never before published in English. It is my contention that the Goths, and the heritage of the Goths, preserve a hidden spiritual treasure that has, up until now, remained buried.

When we hear the word "Gothic" a number of connotations probably spring to mind — Gothic architecture, Gothic romance, Gothic horror — just to name a few. How did the name of an ancient Germanic tribal group become attached to all these cultural and literary features centuries after the Gothic language and people had vanished from the stage of European history? By the end of this book you will have some kind of answer.

The aim and purpose of this book is to begin to unlock the mysteries of the Goths. Every question we have about them can not now be answered, but with the beginning forged in these pages, future radically traditional investigators will be able to delve deeper into the dark corners of the Gothic realm and unlock even more of the mysteries found there.

Certainly this is not the first book or study to attempt a deeper reading of this mysterious history. But it is the only one to focus almost entirely on the Gothic tribes and the Gothic times (pre-711 CE) and not on the later 16th and 17th century obsession with the idea of the Goths especially prevalent in Scandinavia and England. This obsession even has a name— *Gothicism*, "Gothicism" or *Storgoticism*, "Megleo-Gothicism." This movement and its chief esoteric exponent, Johannes Bureus, is the subject of a fine study by Thomas Karlsson, *Adulruna and the Gothic Cabbala*. These early modern Gothic enthusiasts felt that they had discovered the font of all civilization in the ancient Goths. Later in the 18th and 19th centuries Romantics throughout Europe began to identify themselves as "Gothic." The word was applied to all the Germanic peoples— Germans, Anglo-Saxons, as well as all

Scandinavians. These Romantic speculations and aesthetic exercises are not the crux of our study either, although they are discussed more extensively in Appendix B. We want to examine the Gothic mysteries as real mysteries. Too often an aura of "mystery" is created simply for effect, or as a way to conceal or obfuscate the actual roots of an idea. This can be an effective tool in teaching about mystery— about unfolding the noble substance hidden in one's soul— but it can also lead people astray from the actual sources of ideas. Examples of such pseudo-mysteries are things such as Egyptomania (from Plato to modern times) or the Hebrew Kabbalah. Both ancient Egypt and the Hebrew Kabbalah are repositories of their own genuine and authentic traditions and wisdom, but often those from completely outside these traditions project ideas onto these and other "prefabricated models" in order to 1) hide the actual origin of an idea through misdirection and 2) wrap the idea in an aura of prestigious inscrutability. Similar use was made of the undeniable and real myth and historic prestige of the Goths in centuries past. However, in this book our primary focus is on the actual mysteries preserved within the Gothic elite in ancient times— secrets which formed a hidden body of lore among those few nobles who handed it down in an extraordinarily discreet way. The fact that these secrets were indeed preserved, and that attention was for centuries diverted away from this tradition and focused instead on exotic symbols of "the East," "Egypt," etc., can actually lead us back to the true sources and bearers of the secrets. To see beyond the misdirection one must focus initially on the one who gains by conducting the misdirection. We will discover that because the Goths had for centuries been targeted for destruction by the Roman Catholic Church, the direct spiritual and material heir to the Roman Empire, the only mode of survival for the Goths was for them to form a completely hidden tradition. Much has been written in recent years about the landscape of southern France and the so-called mystery of Rennes-le-Château. Misdirection toward the "Celts," the "house of Jesus," the Freemasons, you name it, has been practiced. The Visigoths, who are the obvious focus of attention, and who physically brought "the treasure," which is so much in question, to the region in the first part of the 5th century, are rarely even mentioned at all. This is one of those "touchstones" for unlocking mystery, for bringing the unknown into conscious focus: When the most likely subject (doer) of an action is seen to be systematically shielded by a complex of misdirections then the observer must redouble his efforts to delve behind the shield. Of course, at this particular point in history, this book could not have been written if it were still in the best interests of the Gothic tradition to remain hidden. One of the earliest books to appear on this subject was the 1976 book *Le mystère gothique* by Gérard de Sède. This book touches on some of the points addressed by Sède, but our study goes well beyond his and focuses only on those secret traditions which are firmly attached to the legacy of the ancient Goths, not just various Germanic tribes.

In the course of this book we will first review the general history of the Goths from the time they first step into the historical record around 200 CE to the time of their official demise in western Europe in 711. The history is better and more exhaustively dealt with elsewhere in any of the histories of the Goths found in the bibliography of this book. Therefore, we will concentrate on the historical traditions of the Goths themselves and the cultural, rather than political and military aspects of the secret Gothic tradition. The first of these deals with the mysterious religious traditions of the Goths. The second explores the secrets surrounding the Gothic alphabet invented by Ulfilas to express the Gothic language in writing and its connections both to the ancient runes used by the Goths before Ulfilas and to the Greek mystical traditions linked to the αλφαβητα. The third of these deals with the use of the spear, and more specifically with the symbolic spearheads used as scepters of royal power by the pagan Goths. The fourth delves into several of the mysterious treasures associated with the Goths over the centuries. These include the treasures of Pietroassa, Fuente de Guarrazar, and the greatest of all treasures, the so-called "Temple Treasure" of the Visigoths which disappeared somewhere in southern France. Finally there follows a discussion of various aspects of the legacy of the Goths in the region of southern France related to the people known as the Cagots, and to the so-called mystery of Rennes-le-Château, and all that has come to imply.

At the end of the book there are several appendices which deal with important issues surrounding the mysteries of the Goths ranging from the secret Gothic mission in the world today to the so-called Goth subculture to a short history of the word "Gothic" in English.

The present work unlocks the fundamental secrets of the Goths in a way which will create in the careful and attentive reader a spiritual receptivity to their ancient and timeless message. It is hoped that this book will lead to many others to be written by those who have been able to hear and understand this message. Too often the actual "Gothic gospel" becomes lost in a haze of emotional romance, and the actual secrets stored in the treasure-house remain hidden. Some of the undeniable power of the Goths lies in the fact that after these noble, heroic folk disappeared from the stage of history, suddenly they were transformed into a symbol of the highest aspirations of all of the Germanic tribes. Hence, once there were no more actual Goths, all Germanic peoples — Anglo-Saxons, Germans and Scandinavians — could all become Goths. They were transformed from a particular people into a universal one. The time has come to realize once more the long lost spiritual heritage of the Goths so that its future will be as great and bright as its past.

## Chapter One
# Out of the Womb of Nations

## Historical Frameworks

Historically the Goths emerged from the mists of time and it is into the mist they seem to have evaporated historically. The purpose of our study is to delve into the secrets of the Goths and the mysteries which surround them. But in order to understand fully the context of these more esoteric aspects it is necessary to have some understanding of the exoteric facts having to do with Gothic history, which spanned 700 years and ranged over an entire continent. This history is itself so fascinating and intricate that it would be easy to be swept up in its details. That detailed history is not the mission of this book. I strongly recommend that the serious student acquire and study the texts devoted to Gothic history in order to gain a deeper sense of the historical backdrop of the secrets and mysteries I will be discussing later. However, here I will provide the basic information needed to make sense of Gothic culture and its relations to events in the first several centuries of our era. Many mysteries will be found embedded in what appears to be "ordinary" history.

## Origins of the Goths

No one is exactly sure where the Goths came from. There are definite Gothic traditions about their origins, and archeology has made many inroads into our understanding about their original homeland, but questions remain.

Gothic tradition, recorded in Latin by the 6th century Gothic historian Jordanes, is quite clear about the origin of the Goths. The relevant passage in his *Getica*, or *History of the Goths*, is worthy of quoting:

> IV (25) Now from this island of Scandza, as from a hive of races or a womb of nations, the Goths are said to have come forth long ago under their king, Berig by name. As soon as they disembarked from their ships and set foot on the land, they straightway gave their name to the place. And even to-day it is said to be called Gothiscandza.
>
> (26) Soon they moved from here to the abodes of the Ulmerugi, who then dwelt on the shores of Ocean, where they pitched camp, joined battle with them and drove them from their homes. Then they subdued their neighbors, the Vandals, and thus added to their victories. But when the number of the people increased greatly and Filimer, son of Gadaric, reigned as king--about the fifth since Berig-- he decided that the army of the Goths with their families should move from that region.

> (27) In search of suitable homes and pleasant places they came to the land of Scythia, called Oium in that tongue. Here they were delighted with the great richness of the country, and it is said that when half the army had been brought over, the bridge whereby they had crossed the river fell in utter ruin, nor could anyone thereafter pass to or fro. For the place is said to be surrounded by quaking bogs and an encircling abyss, so that by this double obstacle nature has made it inaccessible. And even to-day one may hear in that neighborhood the lowing of cattle and may find traces of men, if we are to believe the stories of travelers, although we must grant that they hear these things from afar.
> (28) This part of the Goths, which is said to have crossed the river and entered with Filimer into the country of Oium, came into possession of the desired land, and there they soon came upon the race of the Spali, joined battle with them and won the victory. Thence the victors hastened to the farthest part of Scythia, which is near the sea of Pontus; for so the story is generally told in their early songs, in almost historic fashion. Ablabius also, a famous chronicler of the Gothic race, confirms this in his most trustworthy account.

Later Jordanes give us a few more details:

> XVII (94) From this city, then, as we were saying, the Getae returned after a long siege to their own land, enriched by the ransom they had received. Now the race of the Gepidae was moved with envy when they saw them laden with booty and so suddenly victorious everywhere, and made war on their kinsmen. Should you ask how the Getae and Gepidae are kinsmen, I can tell you in a few words. You surely remember that in the beginning I said the Goths went forth from the bosom of the island of Scandza with Berig, their king, sailing in only three ships toward the hither shore of Ocean, namely to Gothiscandza.

From these accounts we learn that Gothic tradition held that the Goths had their original homeland, or *Urheimat*, in Scandinavia. At the time geographers in southern Europe thought that Scandinavia was an island. This "island" could be identified with the Scandinavian peninsula itself, or with the island of Gotland. The reference to Scandinavia being the "womb of nations" indicates the feeling of southern European commentators that great hordes of humanity were pouring out of the north and swarming (like bees) over the Empire. Under their legendary king Berig they are said to land at the mouth of the Vistula, where they founded Gothiscandza, today called Gdansk (German: Danzig). The idea that they made this original voyage in three ships has the ring of symbolic, mythic tradition. Jordanes has the Goths immediately interacting with the "Scythians." Historically it was certainly the Sarmatians and not the Scythians whom the Goths would have encountered.

The Scythians were a north-Iranian horse-based culture whose empire spread from central Asia across the northern shore of the Black Sea and into east-central Europe from around 700 BCE to about 200 BCE. Their name became immortalized in the work of the great Greek historian Herodotus. From then on any nomadic horsemen emerging from the steppes were referred to as "Scythians" by the Greek and Roman historians and ethnographers. Beginning around 200 BCE the Scythians were superseded by the closely related (likewise north-Iranian) Sarmatians. These people were dominant in eastern Europe until the coming of the Goths— with whom they sometimes fought and often merged. Another important northern Iranian culture, that of the Alans, was also present on the steppes and enjoyed a long and productive relationship with the Goths. I will return to a discussion of these tribes later.

The most recent archeological findings have cast doubt on the factual basis of this historical tradition. There is little evidence of an archeological kind to support the idea that a definite distinct people migrated from Scandinavia across the Baltic Sea to the area at the mouth of the Vistula around the beginning of our era. It appears more likely from this sort of evidence that the genesis of the Goths was on the continental shore of the Baltic, in present day northern Poland, rather than in Scandinavia.

On the other hand, traditions such as represented by Jordanes, have often proven to have more factual basis than many have thought. Such traditions, if they are not disqualified as typical non-native interpolations, e.g. stories about "Trojan" or biblical origins, should never be dismissed as meaningless. The conscious symbolic or mythic tradition is always more powerful than the forgotten factual events.

## The Name "Goth"

The name of the Goths is shrouded in mystery. This mystery is only enhanced and deepened by the long history of the name. See Appendix B for more details on this history. One of the main problems is that there were in antiquity a number of different groups and subgroups of people whose names were similar, but not identical, to the name of the Goths.

Tradition has it that they are named after their most distant ancestor, Gaut(s). Some might agree that this eponymous name ws projected back to a myth, however, the probable meaning of the name *Gauts* is something like "father." There is an Icelandic *heiti*, or byname, of Óðinn— Gautr. This element also occurs in the Old Icelandic Rune-Poem in the stanza for *áss* ([god]= Óðinn): *Áss er aldin-gautr*, "God is the ancient father." For more on this poem, see *The Rune Poems* (Rûna-Raven, 2002). This does not necessarily mean that Gauts is identical with Wōðanaz, because the name only means "father," in the etymological sense of of "he who pours out," i.e. the generations or offspring.

From ancient times the name of the Goths appears in a grammatically strong and weak form, *Gut-* and *Guton-* respectively.

Beyond this there is also the fact that the name appears in Greek and Latin as well as Gothic orthographies. Tradition would hold that this name and that contained in the name of Götaland (Götland) in present-day Sweden and the island of Gotland stem from the same source and that these are identical to the Geatas (ON Gautar) in *Beowulf*.

This name later became confused with others. The principal confusion came in connection with the name of a Dacian tribe, the Getae, who inhabited present-day northern Romania at the time the Goths settled there for a short while in the 4th century. These names were then confused by Latin and Greek writers. Through the centuries, as the fame of the Gothic name spread, any similar sounding name came to be identified as "Goth," including the Jutes [yootes] of the North Sea and even the Judaei [yood-ah-ey], "Jews." This confusion with the words beginning with the y-sound came as a result of the palatalization of the letter /g/ in Old English Gēatas [yeatas] and later Scandinavian Götland [yötland]. The link between the name of the Goths and that of the Jews will play a part in some medieval mysteries surrounding the Goths.

Before moving on to the history of the migrations of the Goths southward toward the Black Sea and the Balkans, it is important to discuss the three linguistic or tribal groupings constituting the whole of the Germanic peoples at the time when the Gothic migrations began. From around 700 BCE to shortly after the beginning of our era, the Germanic peoples spoke a more or less single language, called by scholars today Proto-Germanic. These split into three dialect groups called North Germanic (spoken in Scandinavia), West (or south) Germanic (spoken on the Continent roughly west of the Oder) and East Germanic (spoken east of the Oder). Not all of these languages underwent subsequent changes at the same rate. At first the north was most conservative, while change was more rapid in the east. This can be demonstrated with the description of a single well-known word: PGmc. *tīwaz*, the name of the sky-god and the name of the 17th rune in the Older Fuþark. In EGmc. (Gothic) this is *teiws*, in NGmc. *tīwaR* and in SGmc. we find Old High German *ziu* or Old English *tīw*. Here we see that the NGmc., or Primitive Norse, is closest to the original— only the -z has been "rhotacized" to a more *r*-like sound. This, of course, becomes Old Norse Týr. The EGmc. form has transformed the -z into an -s and has lost the so-called thematic vowel -a-. The SGmc. forms show the most radical variations: Old High German *ziu* has 1) lost all inflection in the nominative (subject) grammatical case and 2) has undergone the second German consonantal sound shift whereby the initial *t*- has become a *z*- [tz]. Old English has likewise lost it grammatical ending, but retains the original *t*-sound initially. These technical linguistic details may seem tedious, but they provide some important clues for determining the interactions of various tribes in ancient times and help us to identify certain artifacts of esoteric importance.

In the tribal histories of the Germanic peoples these linguistic designations are also important because they show which tribes shared deep common roots. The East Germanic tribes were, besides the Ostrogoths and Visigoths, the Vandals, the Burgundians, the Gepids and the Rugians. The original homeland of the Burgundians was the island of Bornholm in the Baltic. The Erulians, or Heruli, have also sometimes been classified with the East Germanic "tribes," but their classification remains problematic. Runic inscriptions in the Older Fuþark show that rune-carvers identifying themselves as "Erulians" did not use East Germanic linguistic form, e.g. **ek erilaR**. It is most likely that the Erulians were an intertribal band of oath-bound warriors made up of members of various Germanic tribes.

Generally for purposes of this study we will discuss matters not only pertaining to the Goths, but also to the closely related East Germanic tribes. The Langobards, or Lombards, were a tribe with North Germanic origins who over time adopted the West Germanic dialect during their southward migration and who were close neighbors with East Germanic tribes throughout their history, until they "inherited" domination of northeastern Italy from the vanishing Ostrogoths in the 6th century.

## Early Migrations

For whatever reason the Goths began a southward migration to the borders of the Roman Empire. From their base between the mouths of the Vistula and the Oder, the Goths began to migrate southeastern direction across the steppes beginning around 150 CE. By 170 CE the first wave of Goths had established themselves on the shores of the Black Sea between the mouths of the Don and Dniester. Other waves followed from the north until about 250 CE.

We have already seen how the Gothic historian, Jordanes, describes some of these early migrations. Clearly Jordanes, writing some three centuries after the events as a classically educated man living in Constantinople, is heavily influenced by classical terminology (e.g. the identification of those the Goths encountered on the steppes as "Scythians"). However, that which is not of classical origin in the writings of Jordanes can be thought to represent Gothic tribal tradition, initially recorded in their heroic songs. Jordanes (IV.28) specifically mentions these songs "...for so the story is generally told in their early songs, in almost historic fashion." Most certainly Jordanes had some of these songs, or summaries of them, at his disposal when writing his history, which was based on an older and much longer one by Cassiodorus.

It is likely that the Goths had been interacting with the horse-riding steppe-cultures from the beginning of their history and that when they moved into the then Sarmatian-dominated region in present-day southern Russia, they were already familiar with that culture themselves, having absorbed great numbers of Sarmatians into their ranks and having learned various skills from them. Generally these north-Iranian tribal groups (Sarmatians and Alans) kept separate existences in the ranks of the Goths and never became fully integrated into the Gothic tribes. There was, no doubt, a good deal of intermarriage between these groups at the leading levels of society in order to forge alliances between clans. The dominant language of all of them soon become Gothic, however.

Around 270 the Goths split into two groups— the Visigoths to the west of the Dniester and the Ostrogoths to the east of that river. From this point on these two sub-tribes lead separate destinies. The names are often misinterpreted as meaning West-Goths and East-Goths, respectively. Actually the Visigoths are "the Good and Noble Goths," and Ostrogoths are "the Goths Glorified by the Rising Sun." The element Ostro- refers to the "east" only indirectly as the direction of the rising sun. These two peoples of the Gothic tribe also called themselves the Tervingi ("forest people") and Greutungi ("dwellers of the stepped and pebbly coasts"). (Wolfram, p. 25)

About the division of the Goths into two peoples, and the royal family lines which sustained them and to which they were loyal, Jordanes says of them once they had reached the Balkans:

> (V. 42) ...they had now become more civilized and, as I have said before, were more learned. Then the people were divided under ruling families. The Visigoths served the family of the Balthi and the Ostrogoths served the renowned Amali.
> (43) ...In earliest times they sang of the deeds of their ancestors in strains of song accompanied by the cithara; chanting of Eterpamara, Hanala, Fritigern, Vidigoia and others whose fame among them is great...

## The Hunnic Revolution

It is a mistaken view to place too much emphasis on the invasion of the Gothic territory by the "Huns"— a Turkic group of tribes who was living just to the east of the Alans and Ostrogoths. The Huns were a vigorous, but largely disorganized, people. Reports of them from Roman and Byzantine sources say that they had no real leaders. (Heather, p. 109) They began encroaching on the Ostrogoths in 375 through 376. Although there were significant military struggles, the battle was never one of pure Turkic Huns versus Germanic Goths. The Huns had already become significantly amalgamated with both the

Alanic and Gothic influences. It is most likely that certain Gothic clans or families made early alliances with Hunnic clans, for many well-known Gothic groups, such as the Amal-clan, thrived under Hunnic "domination." The degree to which the Huns were open to foreign influence is reflected in their personal names. A study of these names by Prof. Otto Maenchen-Helfen (pp. 385-442) shows that a surprising percentage of them are of Germanic and Iranian origin, although, of course, their own native Turkic names predominate. Among the Germanic names are Attila. This is a specifically Gothic name. *Atta* is a familiar form of "father," as we see the Gothic translation of the "Lord's Prayer" begins with the phrase *Atta unsar*— "our daddy." To this stem has been added a diminutive suffix, *-ila*. Att-ila means literally "little father." In Russia this remained a way of referring to the czar— e.g. russian *batyushka* or Yiddish *tatila*. Other Germanic names among the Huns cited by Maenchen-Helfen include Edekon, Laudaricus, Onegesius, Ragnaris and Ruga.

By the time the leader named Attila came to power around 440 the amalgamation of Huns, Goths and Alans or Sarmatians had advanced another three generations or so. It has been noted that in medieval secular literary tradition the royal courts of the Hun Attila (434–453) and the Ostrogoth Theodoric the Great (493–526) are *idealized* as paragons of warrior-societies— much like that of King Arthur in Britain. (Edward Haymes *Heroic Legends of the North* [Garland, 1996], p. 3ff.). This reflects a historical secret. The great tradition of aristocratic clanic solidarity and idealized heroic and sovereign virtues remained protected and undisturbed in certain specific lines despite the apparently general chaos of the day. That which lies at the heart of this secret is that which is at the root of the mysteries of the Goths through the ages. This "chaos" and "barbarism" is merely nothing more than Roman — and hence Roman Catholic — contemporaneous and historical propaganda against the people of the North.

## The Ostrogoths

The Hunnic movement into the west first affected the Ostrogoths. Their kingdom along the Black Sea coast was disrupted after the death of their king Ermanaric and the majority of them migrated to the west either ahead of, or along side of, the Huns after 375. However, some Goths remained behind and defended the Crimean Peninsula. These Gothic speakers were occasionally mentioned in history, and the language did not fully die out until the 18th century.

After a relatively brief period in the Balkans, where they participated in the battle of Adrianople (August 9, 378) in which the Goths were victorious over the Romans and their Emperor Valens, who was killed in the battle, they were settled as Roman federates in Panonnia along with the Alans and Huns. The region of Panonnia, present-day Hungary, became an Ostrogothic kingdom from about 451 to 473.

It was there in 454 that Theodoric was born. His father was Theudimir, who ruled the kingdom with his two brothers. At the age of eight Theodoric was given as hostage to the emperor in Constantinople in order to secure a treaty. He remained there for ten years. There Theodoric studied military and political strategy, but ignored his Greek and Latin studies— remaining illiterate. When he was eighteen he was released back to his father. Almost at once Theodoric began gathering and leading his own army. Two years later his father died and the young man was elected king of the Ostrogoths. Although he served the Roman Emperor Zeno in Constantinople well in military affairs, the emperor had reason to fear him. So he gave the Ostrogothic king the mission of conquering Italy, which was at the time dominated by an illegitimate ruler, Odovacer— a Germanic Scirian. Theodoric was promised his own kingdom in what was the heart of the ancient Roman Empire.

In 488 the Ostrogothic people— warriors, women, the elderly and children — began a trek toward Italy. Once in Italy the Ostrogoths under Theodoric allied themselves with the Visigoths and engaged the forces of Odovacer repeatedly in bloody conflicts with Theodoric himself often bravely inspiring his men with acts of courage on the battlefield. Eventually the Ostrogoths laid siege to Ravenna and by the spring of 493 the will of Odovacer has been broken. Theodoric personally killed the tyrant at a banquet he had to which he had invited the vanquished leader.

For several years Theodoric ruled his kingdom peacefully, earning the appellation "the Great." The Ostrogothic king dreamed of a united Europe in which tribes could all live in peace, each respecting the cultural authenticity and legitimacy of the others. Theodoric the Great attempted to bind the various Germanic tribes together and to him through marriage alliances. The king boasted of his educated daughters— learned in Latin and Greek. He promoted the reformation and restoration of economic and juridical order, as well as cultural and architectural development. Roman antiquities which had fallen into disrepair were restored by him.

Theodoric did practice a kind of apartheid policy with regard to the Goths and Romans. Each group was to remain separate, each fulfilling a certain purpose. The Goths defended the land and the Romans administered it. Such success could not go unchallenged by the Roman Catholics or by the Byzantine Emperor.

Clovis (Choldwig), king of the Franks, converted to Roman Catholicism in 496, although he may not have been formally baptized until 508. He was the first Germanic king to become fully Romanized willingly. He did so in order to form an alliance with the Catholic

Church and the Byzantine Emperor against the cultural foe all of them feared— the Goths. Toward the end of his reign the alliances Theodoric had carefully built up to ensure peace were systematically undermined by Frankish-Catholic-Byzantine interests. Conspiracies were launched in the court of the great Gothic king as well. Eventually it appears that Theodoric was poisoned by agents of the Catholic Church on the day he decided to confiscate their church property in his kingdom. The date was August 30, 526.

Theodoric was idealized by the Germanic tribes well beyond the Goths. But for the Roman Catholics he was a diabolical figure. This dichotomy of attitudes is reflected in the myths which grew up around the circumstances following his death, as his body disappeared from his mausoleum.

> Bizarre new legends were then born: for the Catholics, a great black horse (the devil) stole the body and took it to the mouth of Vulcan into which Theodoric fell (inferno); for the Germanic tribes, Theodoric was taken away by a great horse (belonging to Odin) and transported still alive to be with the heroes in Valhalla.
> (Salti, p. 21)

The mausoleum which Theodoric's body was initially entombed is itself a Gothic mystery. It stands today in all its pristine and austere glory. Theodoric himself has a hand in its design. It is intended to reflect the Gothic tribal aesthetic in contrast to the Roman-style of his *public* building projects. Soon after entombment, the body of the king disappeared.

Wolfram concludes regarding the pagan North's attitude toward Theodoric and his death:
> Nobody knows who removed Theodoric from his final resting place. Of course, in the eyes of the barbarian world the Gothic king had never died: fully armed he sat on his charger, ready to lead the demonic army of the dead, or as the god of war, to receive the sacrifices of the warriors. (Wolfram, p. 332)

The Ostrogothic kingdom built by Theodoric would endure twenty-six more years. Eventually the Goths of Italy would fade from history, but they left their legacy in the subcultural stream of prestige which remains to this day.

# The Visigoths

The Visigoths had lived in closer proximity to the Roman Empire for a longer period of time than the Ostrogoths before the latter group was displaced by the Huns. Therefore the Visigoths were dealing with the Eastern Roman Empire in the cultural sphere from the early 4th century. As discussed in more detail in the next chapter, it was among the Visigoths that Bishop Ulfilas was active as a missionary for his "semi-Arian" form of Christianity. This missionary work was resisted by the leader of the Visigoths, Athanaric.

As the Huns put pressure on the Visigoths, they divided into two camps. One remained north of the Danube under Athanaric, who retreated before the Huns, the other was the one that crossed into the Empire under Fritigern in 375. But after Fritigern's death in 380, Athanaric was named king over all the Visigoths. Athanaric remained a figure of pagan legend because of his general opposition to the Christianization of the Goths on the grounds that it would eventually lead to their Romanization and loss of tribal solidarity. It seems that Athanaric opposed Christianity as a Roman cultural influence on the one hand, and also from a political/religious viewpoint. He saw the separation of religion from the other aspects of life, something implicit in Christianity as a "world-rejecting" ideology, as detrimental to the pubic good of his Goths.

The Visigoths were slowly pressed from their homeland south of the Dnestr river to an area on the border of the Roman Empire on the north shore of the lower Danube around 375 CE. They were admitted into the Empire by the Emperor Valens the next year, when many moved south of the Danube into the Empire proper. When, in 378, there was a shortage of supplies for the Goths, they rebelled against the Empire and inflicted a great military defeat on the Romans at the battle of Adrianople, in which the Emperor Valens was killed.

After this period they resettled further to the west and came under the leadership of Alaric, who became their king. He subsequently led them on migratory campaigns in the Balkans and on into Italy. During his campaign in Italy, Alaric sacked the City of Rome. The Visigoths entered the city on August 24, 410, and left three days later. Their destruction was light; however, they did plunder the entire Roman treasury— perhaps the greatest mass of gold in the world at the time. Shortly after this historic event, Alaric died in southern Italy. It had been his plan to take his people across the Mediterranean into North Africa.

The successors to Alaric moved the Visigoths back northward into Italy and eventually westward. By 412 they were in what is now southern France, and by 419 they had firmly established their own kingdom based around the city of Toulouse. The Kingdom of Toulouse was powerful and prosperous, and endured from 419 to 507. It stretched from central Gaul (France) to central Spain. This kingdom, which was an enclave of the Arian religious heresy, was defeated at the battle of Vouillé in 507 by the Franks under clovis. Clovis had forged an alliance with the Roman Church in an effort to defeat his powerful Visigothic rivals.

After 507 the Visigothic kingdom was reduced to is possessions south of Toulous in what is now Spain and extreme southwestern France. This kingdom, with its capital in Toledo, lasted until the Muslim conquest of the Kingdom of Toledo in 711. One of the most significant cultural events in the history of this Visigothic kingdom was the conversion of king Rekkared to Roman Catholicism in 586. This moment brought to an end the Gothic religious segregation from the rest of Europe, a segregation which had been based on a profound symbolic distinction. It was during this Catholic period that the Visigothic kings had votive crowns made of gold which were displayed in the church. After 711 many of the Goths retreated just to the north. Two more kings were elected by the Visigoths, but they had no integral kingdom to govern.

Despite these events, the Visigothic heritage and legacy in Spain was not wiped out because the Muslim conquest of the Iberian Peninsula was never quite complete. Areas in far northwestern Spain (Asturia) and along the Pyrenees, the so-called Spanish March, including the Kingdom of Navarre and the County of Barcelona, remained free from the Muslim Emirate of Cordoba. It was from these remnants that the lng campaign of *Reconquesta* took place. This "reconquest" was not complete until 1492.

It is customary to measure the "official" end of Gothic history in western Europe with the year 711. However, the legacy and heritage of the Gothic idea was so powerful that it endured in many places long after that date.

## The Gothic Legacy

Because the Goths made such a profound impression on the history of western and southern Europe — along with many other Germanic tribes from the north — memory of them runs deep throughout all of Europe. Additionally, because their prestige was extremely high among the northern Europeans as well as among certain groups in the south, their historical legacy was persistent well beyond the chronological limits of the political power of the actual Gothic tribes. The Goths were the great conquerers, those who "defeated" Rome (by sacking the Eternal City itself), those who set up the first independent national kingdoms in Europe rising from the rubble of the Roman Empire. The reputation of the Goths was by no means entirely positive, however. By many Roman Catholics, who derived their cultural prestige from their association with the idea of Rome, from *Romanitas*, the Goths were symbolically seen as the spoilers of civilization, as wild barbarians bent on pillage and plunder. The Vandals, an allied East Germanic people, were later saddled with some of these (usually undeserved) negative associations— hence the modern word "vandalism" to describe wanton acts of destruction. In fact, of course, the Goths as well as Vandals generally had a humanizing influence on the decadent and anomic Roman culture, restoring law and order and closing down Roman arenas where murder and animal cruelty were practiced for entertainment purposes. Again the negative assessment of the "barbaric" Goths stems almost entirely from proponents of Christian *Romanitas* in an effort to secure their own political power and prestige.

These efforts to suppress the Gothic heritage were to a great extent successful when we view them over the broad spectrum of history. But the truth of the Gothic character and its achievements was kept alive like a secret flame in the hearts of certain groups of nobles as well as in secret enclaves of the church from the ancient homelands in the north to Spain, and from Italy to England.

Much of the Gothic legacy is political in nature. The Goths introduced and maintained particular political ideas and structures in certain areas of Europe, and even after several centuries these have left their marks. Already in the late Middle Ages we see clear evidence of the persistence of Gothic political prestige when the records of a Roman Catholic ecclesiastical conference which met in Basel in 1434 reflect that representatives from several nations, e.g. Sweden and Spain, argued for more influence at the conference due to their ancestral connections to the exalted Gothic race. The Swedish representative, Nicolaus Ragvaldi argued that Sweden was the original homeland of the Goths, while the Spanish representative countered that the Spanish Goths more perfectly demonstrated the adventurous Gothic spirit of courage by migrating away from their homeland than the Swedish Goths who stayed behind like cowards. This testimony is the clearest direct evidence of the degree to which Gothic political and cultural prestige was still alive and vital a *full eight hundred years* after the official demise of the Goths in Spain.

After the fall of the Roman Empire the political map of Europe was largely redrawn under the direct influence of the migratory patterns of the Germanic tribes. The later nations of Spain and Italy first took post-imperial shape under the political guidance of the Gothic kings. Other East Germanic tribes, the Vandals and Burgundians, left their names on regions in Europe, Andalusia in Spain and Burgundy in France, receptively. The spelling "Andalusia" is the result of the fact that in arabic no initial *v*- sound is possible. Additional examples of Germanic tribal names which left their marks on southern Europe include France (< *Francia*, "land of the Franks"), Lombardy in Italy (from the tribal name of the Langobards, "long-beards") and Normandy in France (from "North-men").

An additional Gothic political theory which has had some continuity is the segregationist policy of Theodoric the Great in Italy. This policy was not established by the Ostrogothic king in order to exclude Romans from power or to ensure Gothic supremacy, but rather to preserve the integrity and cultural authenticity of Roman and Goth alike and to maintain the solidarity and survival of the Gothic minority in Italy. This early form of apartheid was successful only during the reign of Theodoric. Eventually the Roman Catholic majority overwhelmed the Arian Goths. But it remains a Gothic idea to preserve the integrity and authenticity of cultural groups through separation within the state in which each group fulfills certain functions for the whole.

Besides these political legacies, the Goths left behind a number of cultural features and patterns which would survive or be emulated over the centuries. Their Arianism would be revisited by theologians many times over the centuries. More will be said about this later. At this point it is sufficient to say that the fundamental principle that Jesus was a man who became godlike, a principle which seems supported by an objective reading of the texts of Christian mythology, opens the door to a more humanistic form of Christianity. The architectural style called "Gothic" was certainly something never practiced by the actual migratory Gothic tribes. However, the general sprit of that architecture does stem from the north of Europe, imbued with Gothic vitality.

The Goths were well-remembered in the poetic and epic literatures of later Germanic peoples. For example, the Old English poem "Widsiþ" (ca. 7th century) records the heroic exploits of the Gothic kings who "with their tough swords had to defend their ancient ancestral homeland seat near the Vistula Forest against the people of Attila." Much of the Nibelung-cycle concerns itself with the interaction of East Germanic Burgundians and the Huns. While the Dietrich-cycle of epics, most extensively recorded in the Norse translation of a Low German original text entitled the *Þiðrekssaga*, recounts the legendary court of Theodoric (= Dietrich).

That this literature is no mere frivolous entertainment for kings, but rather is a reflection of deep mythic concerns, is demonstrated by the text of the runic inscription on the Rök stone (ca. 825 CE) in Sweden, which reads in part:

| | |
|---|---|
| Theodoric the bold | king of sea-warriors |
| at one time ruled | on the reið-shores. |
| Now he sits armed | on his Gothic (horse), |
| the first of heroes | his shield on a strap. |

This poetic stanza shows the mytho-magical reverence in which the figure of Theodoric was held, not only among the Goths, but throughout the Germanic world.

The power of the Goths hinges on their tremendous prestige. The power of prestige is the most powerful single factor in the maintenance of cultural continuity and integrity, as well as the process of cultural change. In the south the Gothic brought stability and order to a crumbling, chaotic Empire which had lost its nerve and vigor. Thus they enjoyed great prestige among a certain segment of the populations of those countries. Their continuing prestige in the north provided an ample measure of cultural continuity in those countries. Additionally, where the Gothic became firmly entrenched, most notably on the Iberian peninsula, where they held sway for the better part of three centuries, the prestige of the Goths provided the mythic strength for the Spaniards to reconquer that land from the Muslim invaders.

The prestige of the Gothic identity was important in royal circles from Spain to Sweden. Such prestige focused both inwardly, where identity with the Gothic provided confidence and solidarity, and outwardly, where it distinguished those who possessed this identity from those who did not possess it. This further intensified the group's sense of solidarity and integrity.

This prestige certainly had a metaphysical dimension as well. Gothic identity was not merely a random or arbitrary thing. It implied a degree of greatness, and bore a whole series of ideological traits as well: *freedom, independence, heroism, individualism within group solidarity.*

Moreover, as will be seen in subsequent chapters, this original Gothic prestige also found its way into lower social strata into which historical Gothic remnants appear to have been submerged. While kings tended to identify with with the Gothic heritage in Spain, in southern France, where Gothic royalty had been replaced by a Frankish one, the remnants of the Gothic population increasingly tended to fade into the social and regional "under-classes" — peasants and craftsmen — who were thus greatly influenced by Gothic traits.

Much of this Gothic prestige is clearly traceable in the degree to which Gothic and Germanic *personal names* are found among the Spaniards and Italians. The Spanish surname Rodriguez is derived from Rodrigo/Roderik, the last Gothic king of Spain. Many first names are of Germanic and even specifically Gothic origin, e.g. Alberto, "bright nobility," Adolfo, "noble wolf," Alfredo, "elven-counsel," Alfonso, "noble and ready," Amalia, "work," Anselmo, "helm of god," Armando, "army man," Enrice, "home ruler," Geraldo, "brave spear," Carlos, "man, farmer," Hermenegildo, "great sacrifice," Ildefonso, "battle ready," Matilda, "strength in battle," Rosendo, "path of fame," Tancredo, "counsel of thought." These lists of names show the degree to which Gothic and Germanic names either survived, or were revived in areas where the Goths held sway in the early Middle Ages. The fact that the names are so *popular* indicates again how prestigious the Gothic and Germanic heritage was in these areas.

The history of the Goths is fairly well documented, However, this documentation can be deceptive in that it is almost entirely written by non-Goths. It also focuses on military and political affairs and pays little attention to cultural matters and the actual living values of the people.

As the Goths slipped away from the historical record in the 8th century, they and their values and principles increasingly became part of a secret European tradition which carried forth the Gothic ideal. Only occasionally during the next millennium would the Gothic ideal become conscious in the societies which inherited their lineages. This book is not so much a history of the revival of the Gothic ideal as it is a delineation of what those Gothic ideals actually were and what they perennially continue to be.

## History of the Gothic Tradition
## Exoteric and Esoteric

The Gothic spiritual or mythic tradition exists in the world on two levels, an exoteric one — which is the documented history of the Goths and their practices and beliefs as they existed in history — and an esoteric one— which is the secret tradition surrounding the Goths. The latter is only sporadically documented and exists as a sort of shadow of the visible exoteric tradition.

### Exoteric

Historically we see that the Goths, an East Germanic tribe, emerged out of the north around 150 CE and began to migrate through present-day Russia bringing with them a pagan religious tradition. Some of them converted to Christianity beginning in the middle of the 4th century, but this process of Christianization was conditioned by two factors: 1) the form of Christianity was not orthodox and thus it remained independent of certain non-Gothic influences, and 2) the secular court-culture of the kings and warriors remained largely aloof from this influence. This latter point is the key to the continuation of the esoteric tradition beyond the limits of historical constraints. The Gothic Christian tradition was maintained and promoted externally by Gothic kings in the 5th and 6th centuries. The exoteric tradition died out in Italy in the 6th century, but continued until the 8th century among the Visigoths in southern France and northern Spain. The official conversion of the Visigoths to Roman Catholicism in 589 fundamentally transformed this tradition. The Islamic invasion of Spain in 711 displaced the Goths to the far northern parts of the country, where, by the mid-700s they seem to have lost their distinctive culture as far as any outward signs are concerned.

### Esoteric

The Gothic royal families maintained, from the time of their origins in Scandinavia and the Baltic, secret tribal traditions. It is these secrets which account for their success and the immortality of their name. These traditions hinged on the continuing secret cult of *divine ancestry*— the hidden cult of the *anseis*. The formula *divine ancestry* must be understood *both* its parts. First the idea is that there is a divine — immortal, perfect and wise — component or element or substance which is not bound by time or place. This transcends the mundane world— stands above it. Second is the idea that this substance can be transmitted or transferred from person to person, or from generation to generation, through historical time and over natural space. We know that this ancestral portion could be transmitted genetically (through the blood), or through symbolic initiations (blood-brotherhood, adoption, reception into warrior-bands, guilds, etc.). Although these latter methods were well-known to the pagans and well-documented among them, it appears that under the influence of the Christian tradition of "apostolic succession" these latter methods grew to be more and more prestigious over the centuries. This increasingly became the method whereby the threatened esoteric of the Goths could be secretly transmitted— and thus protected from an ever more hostile world.

Another important factor in the esoteric tradition is the well-known constant interaction between the Gothic realms of the south and the ancient homelands in Scandinavia and other points in far northern Europe. Cultural and economic contact was maintained and on occasion marriage partners were exchanged between the northern and southern realms as well.

The high-points of the secret tradition are two: 1) the kingship of Theodoric the Great and 2) the Visigothic kingdoms of Toulouse and Toledo.

Up until the time of the general demise of the Gothic kingdoms, the esoteric aspects of Gothic culture are extremely difficult to trace simply because these cultural features were so well concealed within an established and secure tradition. But after the eventual collapse of the external, or exoteric, Gothic social order, the directions in which these esoteric features went in order to preserve themselves make the picture a bit clearer. It must be remembered that the ancient Gothic traditions had had centuries of survival in relatively hostile environments, so its practitioners were well-versed in the arts of concealment and secret transmission.

The traditions in question were reestablished — imperfectly and in some cases only temporarily to be sure — in three different areas of society: the nobility, the church and the peasantry (or other "outcast" groups).

Somewhat ironically, the nobility, where the ancient traditions had customarily been preserved most assiduously, proved to be the most fragile matrix for their continuation after the disestablishment of the Gothic hegemony. The reason for this is that the houses or families bearing the tradition — ones with real political, economic and military power — were obviously constantly the targets of aggression by other forces desirous of their power. Therefore these progressively dispossessed families were either annihilated entirely, or, once they had lost their noble status, carried on as (often fairly well-to-do) farmers or tradesmen. A similar process occurred with the Anglo-Saxon nobility after the the Norman Conquest.

In Italy the Ostrogothic remnants attached themselves to the Langobards, who invaded and settled in the very heartland of Ostrogothic Italy in the last half of the 6th century. That region is still known by the name "Lombardy"— the land of the Langobards. The Goths and Longobards had, of course, long been familiar with one another as fellow migratory tribes from the far north. In Spain, following the (partial) Islamic conquest, the remnants of noble Gothic families established themselves for a while in far northern Iberia and around the Pyrenees on the border between Spain and France. There the kingdoms of Castile (later divided into Aragón, Navarre and Castile) was established, but it eventually fell under French domination in the 13th century. As a general rule, the royal houses proved to be unreliable repositories of the Gothic tradition, as their main interest after the conversion to Roman Catholicism was increasingly one of mere political expediency.

Again ironically, it was the matrix of the Roman Catholic Church itself which proved to be the more stable conduit for Gothic traditions in the Middle Ages. This is simply because the church was an institution based on some tradition, and if a secret enclave could establish itself in certain localities (almost parasitically) within the church, it could survive for a long period. The secret Gothic traditions tended to gather themselves around the towns and cities in southern France which were sites of Visigothic churches— such as perhaps Rennes-le-Château.

At this point a preliminary note should be added about the whole craze surrounding southern France in general, Rennes-le-Château in specific, and the whole "holy blood, holy grail/Da Vinci code complex." One glaring reality must be confronted: The region is most marked by a Visigothic heritage. If a great treasure existed in the region, it is the wealth of the Roman treasury brought by the descendants of Alaric which is the only candidate which explains the enormity and persistence of the legends. Celts had inhabited the region in antiquity, but it was not a thriving center for them. Neither was it extremely important to the Romans. With the arrival of the Visigoths, however, the landscape and populace were impressed with certain special properties. Visigothic churches and fortresses and their arrangement were parts of the complex, as were the traditions carried in families, secret enclaves within the churches as well as in the peasantry. The idea that this region has much to do with Frankish Merovingian tradition, as proposed most famously in the book *Holy Blood, Holy*

*Grail* and in subsequent literature, is almost absurd. First of all, the Merovingians are latecomers to the region, which had been established as the Kingdom of Toulouse by the Visigoths. It will be recalled that the Franks became Roman Catholics in order to enter into an alliance with the Roman Church against the Goths and were the chief opponents of the secret ancestral traditions of the Goths. The founder of the Merovingians, Merovech, probably flourished around 450 CE, long after the establishment of the key Gothic traditions in question. One book, *The Templars' Secret Island* (Barnes and Noble, 2002) shows supposed similarities between the sacred landscape around Rennes-le-Château in southern France and the island of Bornholm in the Danish archipelago. The patterns may be legitimate, but the underlying theory of the book appear to be a misdirection, as are all of the *Holy Blood, Holy Grail* theoretical offshoots. In fact there were no Templars ever recorded on the island of Bornholm at any time. Bornholm, as we have seen, was the ancestral home of the Burgundians, an East Germanic tribe closely allied with the Goths. The Burgundians have left their name on the southern French landscape in the region known today as Burgundy. It is this ancestral and organic connection which is ultimately responsible for the patterns on the landscape — not some farfetched theory which as farfetched as it seems nevertheless serves conventional reality — that there are connections with "Old Testament" mythology or that of Egypt, etc.

Within the Roman Catholic Church, at the level of the local parish churches, the old Visigothic traditions were sometimes preserved in secret. These traditions, along with the actual church buildings which housed them, slowly deteriorated over the centuries. By the 19th century most of these churches had been rebuilt or were in ruins. This is perhaps the source of the famous "Visigothic pillar" which was set up at the Church of Ste Marie Madeleine at Rennes-le-Château, and which is now in a local museum. Enclaves within the local church carried on secret traditions largely unrelated to any church dogma or doctrine— as it had to do with the sacred layout of the landscape, the location of certain treasure hoards, and the core of the mystery— the fact that a royal blood flowed in the veins of certain families— the blood of the *anseis*, the divine ancestors. This idea was perverted by the adherents of the Roman Church, most usually for *monetary* gain, into the notion of the "royal blood" of Jesus, etc. The idea that Jesus never died, but lived on as a teacher and secret king would appeal to an Arian (Gothic) Christian in ways it would not to an orthodox Roman Christian. In fact such an idea negates Roman Catholic dogma in every respect. For Roman Catholic dogma, linked as it is to Old Testament "prophecy," Jesus must die (be sacrificed) in order to fulfill his mission. However, for the Goth the power of the Lord (*Frauja*) to save mankind was not in his death, but in his living teaching which has remained secret.

The whole literature on the "Holy Blood, Holy Grail" mythos and the mysteries of Rennes-le-Château is in need of revalorization with closer attention to historical facts, and with an eye toward the unknown, rather than various hoaxes and mere propaganda for the "conventional mysteries." Our present study is not focused on this, but such a study would be most welcome.

Finally, the esoteric legacy of the Goths in the peasants and commoners in southern France and northern Spain must be addressed. The old nobility, as it was displaced over time in the 8th-10th centuries, was submerged into the local population of commoners and even peasants. Some were displaced into families of Jews— with whom the Goths had sometimes been confused by the Romans and by Roman Catholic Christians. As they ceased being the warriors they had been, these Gothic cultural refugees took up various crafts, such as stone masonry. In chapter 6 we will return to specific instances of possible Gothic survivals in the subcultures of southern France and in connection with the Knights Templar.

In order to appreciate fully the degree and level to which the Gothic tradition was able to survive as a highly esoteric teaching throughout hundreds of years of history, one must realize that it purposefully was projected into three functional streams: 1) priests, 2) warriors, and 3) peasants/craftsmen. Those who are aware of the three functions of the archaic Indo-European religious and social system will at once recognize the meaning and utility of this projection.

It is now time for us to turn to the deeper substance of the esoteric traditions as they were preserved in practical forms in different vehicles within the established Gothic culture.

Chapter Two

# Mysteries of the Gothic Church

The greatest mysteries and esoteric lore surrounding the Goths stem from their tribal ideology and its various forms of expression throughout history. To understand these mysteries to any degree it is most necessary to cast our gaze into the origins of the Goths and to their tribal, pre-Christian, traditions. These remain obscure due to the fact that no autochthonous pagan Gothic source has survived, other than a runic inscription or two. Some scholars in the early 20th century, however, believed that the bulk of Eddic mythology actually stemmed from the Goths. It is certainly true that much of the heroic material in the *Edda* rises out of the Gothic cultural melieu. Beyond this it is imperative to grasp the history and tenets of the unique form of Gothic Christianity which so marked and distinguished them throughout most of their history. This leads us to discover some of the esoteric aspects of the Gothic legacy. It is most likely that much of the modern-day mythic lore surrounding the southern French (Provincial) landscape — most notably Renne-le-Château — actually has roots in the legendary past of the Goths and that other more "far fetched" explanations or theories are merely more culturally acceptable affinities. Realizing this opens a whole new door to investigation.

## The Ancient Gothic Religion

Because there is no "Gothic Edda," it is difficult to unravel what the finer details of Gothic pagan tradition was. However, enough clues have been left behind in various scattered sources to make a good reconstruction possible. To this must also be added the comparative evidence of what we know about the general proto-Germanic world out of which the Goths migrated and in which their roots still lie.

Perhaps the most complete and thorough exploration of what could be called Gothic paganism was offered by the German historian of religion, Karl Helm, in the third volume of his *Altgermanische Religionsgeschichte* (1937).

After the Goths were nominally Christianized, the nobility still held onto the old traditions for a much longer time. Christianity first developed in the Gothic realms among foreigners and slaves, just as it had among the Romans. Therefore the kings embraced it only slowly and kept many aspects of it at arms length, simply because it theoretically diminished their power.

## The Spiritual World

To understand the spiritual universe of a people one must understand some essential parts of it and from these parts synthesize the whole in some inner way. Otherwise we just collect isolated and virtually meaningless facts with which we have no empathy, and hence no real understanding is possible. One of the most important areas of life which must be understood, especially for archaic or traditional peoples is their *soul conceptions*. Modern man has largely lost any intuitive knowledge of this part of himself. He has had to rely on the reconstructed discipline of "psychology" to recover (haphazardly) a small portion of what our ancestors knew and used intuitively on a daily basis. These conceptions are best rediscovered through a detailed structural and etymological analysis of the words making up the terminology for this area of life. In connection with this we can examine the funerary rites of the Goths to see how, at the end of life, these parts of the whole person are dealt with.

## Soul Conceptions

In the case of the Old Norse terminology for the soul we have the advantage of thousands of pages of text which provide authentic context for the various terms in question. We have humans motivated by, and interacting with, these concepts in a variety of situations. In the case of Gothic we have a much more archaic level of attestation, however, the whole of the material is recorded entirely within a Christianized context. This has its advantages and disadvantages. Its disadvantages are obvious, however, we do get in the case of the Gothic terms clear and definite Greek translations of the terms, which open another door to the understanding of the concepts.

Gothic *ahma* (Gk. πνευμα [*pneuma*]) is derived from the Proto-Germanic root *\*ah-* with the suffix *-ma*, which makes it into a collective and abstract meaning. *\*Ah-* by itself relates to the idea of "reflecting, pondering." This root is also found in OE *eaht*, "deliberation," OHG *ahta*, "thought," and in the ON verb *ætla*, "to think, mean, suppose." Clearly it originally had a cognitive, thinking component, but the use of it to translate Greek πνευμα, "spirit" indicates that for Ulfilas it had connotations of "spirituality" for him that went beyond mere cogitation. Originally this would have been the breath of life and divinity breathed into the human being by the gods.

A second Gothic term, *aha*, is used to translate the Greek νους, which clearly indicates the original cognitive, thinking aspect of the root concept *\*ah-*. In Greek the νους (*nous*) is the mind proper. Although other Germanic languages have psychological terms also derived from the root *\*ah-*, Gothic is the only dialect which has developed this root into a true soul conception.

The Gothic word *hugs* is also used to translate the Greek νους, and it is this root, **hug*-, which is the most widely attested Germanic term for the cognitive aspect of the human soul. We see it also in ON *hugr*, OHG *hugu*, OS *hugi*, OE *hige*, all meaning "mind, spirit, hear, etc." The ultimate etymology of this word is uncertain, but it most likely goes back to the Proto-Indo-European root *keuk*-, "to shine." Hence we still say of a person who we think is intelligent, that he or she is "bright." The cognitive part of the soul is that part of us which processes data, especially data which is seen to emerge from the outside world, in a logical or rational manner.

A contrasting concept is denoted by the Gothic words *gaminþi* or *gamunds*, which translate variously the Greek terms μνεια, μνημοσυνη, 'αναμσησις, all of which indicate "memory." This part of the soul indicates that faculty which reflects on the internal, subjective contents of the mind. This is reflective, rather than cognitive. To the traditional Germanic mind this suggested that the things contemplated by the *gamunds* were, or could be, things received from deep inside the mind or spirit originally breathed into man by the gods, or to be the contents of a "divine mind." Hence, in the Norse Hávamál (st. 20) we read how the god Óðinn, who has two ravens named after the two mental faculties of mind (Huginn) and memory (Muninn), fears more for the loss of Muninn (memory) than he does for Huginn (mind). The *hugs* is more conscious, the *gamunds* more unconscious.

Another part of the conscious mind, *wilja*, "the will" is used by Ulfilas to translate the Greek term θελημα (*thelēma*), which is largely a New Testament term. Gothic *wilja* was originally a strong desire, a force of focus and direction to the human mind to make plans and see them through to their completion. The older, pre-Christian, term for this faculty of the human mind in Greek was βουλη (*būlē*). Interestingly enough, βουλη is also one of the Greek words Ulfilas translates with Gothic *rūna*, "secret, mystery."

The Gothic word *saiwala* is used to translate the Greek word ψυχη (*psychē*) which is used very frequently in the New Testament. In Greek it originally referred to the "breath," and to the "departed soul" of a person. In specifically Christian terminology *psychē* was translated as "soul," while *pneuma* denoted "spirit." In pre-Christian terms the *saiwala* was the part of the person which departed after death and took on an independent existence, either in the realm of the dead (e.g. ON Hel) or in a higher realm (e.g. ON Valhöll). In the former case the soul was likely to be reborn in to the clan naturally, whereas in the latter case the soul would take on a more or less permanent existence in the higher world.

These various soul-conceptions are laid out in a structural format in figure 3.1. Such formats are intended to suggest the relationships of the various concepts one to the others, but in fact, of course, these categories of being exist in a realm which is impossible to "diagram" in models making use of two or even three dimensions. Material relating to the Gothic tradition should be compared to that of the other (especially the Norse) Germanic terminologies in order to understand the Gothic mind thoroughly. A convenient represtatation of the Norse material can be found in *Runelore* by Thorsson (Weiser, 1987, pp. 167-173)

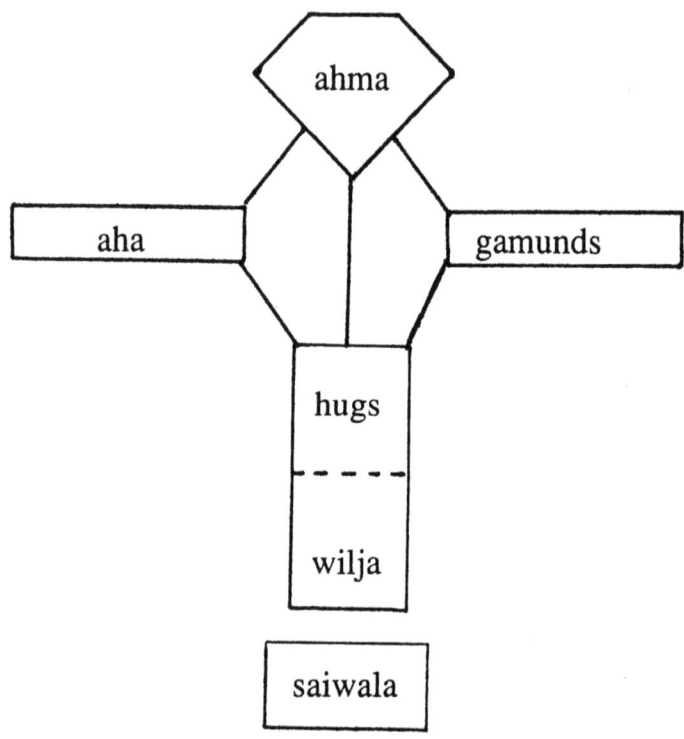

Figure 3.1: The Configuration of the Gothic Soul

## Funerary Customs

In the absence of autochthonous texts one of the ways to discover something of the indigenous ideas about the soul is to analyze the various ways in which the bodies of the dead were treated. From early on it appears that the Goths practiced a mixture of inhumation (burial) and cremation (burning) the bodies of the dead. In the case of cremation, the ashes were usually subsequently buried in urns. It also appears, however, that the Goths gave up the practice of cremation fairly early on. (Helm, pp. 10-11)

Both inhumantion and cremation aim to achieve similar goals in the Germanic culture. Inhumation returns the body to the earthly, or chthonic realm, through the slow decomposition of the body in Mother Earth. While cremation effects an immediate and dramatic decomposition of the elements of the body by fire and returns it to Father Sky. In general cremation was preferred by warriors and kings of the second and first functions in Indo-European times. But in either case grave mounds could be erected as memorials to the dead ancestor.

In ancient times graves most typically had what are called "grave goods" deposited in them. These are objects, practical and symbolic, which are placed in the grave so that the departed will have use of them in the next world. Most typically, warriors would have weapons, etc. However, in the case of the Goths it has been noticed that their inhumation graves have no weapons as grave goods. (Helm p. 12ff.) On the other hand, the Vandals, a related East Germanic tribe did have weapons as grave goods. It appears that the Goths, although often a warlike people in the earthly world, emphasized the idea of the warriors' paradise less than other East Germanic peoples did.

Ammatas Procopius (*De bello Vandalico* I,21) reports that there was still the practice of cremation in special circumstances among the Goths. The Eruli (*De bello Goth.* II, 14) are said to kill and burn the sick and old. Sidionius Apollinaris (*Epist.* 3,3 [470]) says that the Visigoths burned their dead in their wagons after the battle of Clermont against Ecdicius.

Gothic history provides several examples of famous funerals given to various well-known individuals which we can examine for more information.

After his untimely death, the Visigothic king Alaric was buried in Italy. Jordanes (XXX.158) describes the circumstances of his funeral as follows:

> His people mourned for him with the utmost affection. Then turning from its course the river Busentus near the city of Consentia--for this stream flows with its wholesome waters from the foot of a mountain near that city--they led a band of captives into the midst of its bed to dig out a place for his grave. In the depths of this pit they buried Alaric, together with many treasures, and then turned the waters back into their channel. And that none might ever know the place, they put to death all the diggers. They bestowed the kingdom of the Visigoths on Athavulf his kinsman, a man of imposing beauty and great spirit; for though not tall of stature, he was distinguished for beauty of face and form

We will discuss the idea of the treasure of Alaric in much more detail in chapter 4.

The burial of Attila is also reported by Jordanes (XLIX.256ff.) in some detail. It seems to have many Gothic characteristics, which is only fitting as much of his army was actually made up of Goths and other East Germanic tribesmen.

In the most traditional circumstances the Goths would be expected to raise an earthen mound over the body and funerary goods of the dead. One of the most extraordinary structures of the ancient world is the tomb of Theodoric the Great in Ravenna. This tomb, the structural mysteries of which still await a fuller analysis, is an architectural version of the same idea conveyed by the ancient grave-mound. As the historical circumstances of the death of Theodoric and the subsequent quick disappearance of his body from the tomb show, the tomb was never able to be used in the manner for which it was obviously designed. This purpose was an elaborate form of ancestor worship. The tomb held the body in a sarcophagus in the lower level of the structure, and above this was a level containing a space, with no apparent access from the inside in ancient times, in which rites of ancestor worship were to be performed by the descendants of Thoedoric the Great. This perfectly reflects the ancient practice of the Germanic peoples in which rites were held either in front of, or on top of, earthen grave mounds.

Tomb of Theodoirc the Great in Ravenna, Italy

As a side note it should be perhaps be pointed out that the killing of "slaves" at the burial of Attila and Alaric as reported by Jordanes was probably not motivated by the prevention of such slaves from betraying the site of the burial. It is rather more likely that this was a reflection of the old practice of sacrificing slaves and prisoners of war as a part of the funerary rite in pagan times. This practice is more elaborately described in the *Travel Report of Ibn Fadlan* (Rûna-Raven, 1998, pp. 8-11).

## Spirits and Demons

In addition to humans, there is also a variety of beings which are thought to inhabit the world alongside living humans. Some of these are malevolent, or dangerous to humans, while others are more neutral. Perhaps the most famous example of demonic entities being mentioned in Gothic history occurs in Jordanes' history (XXIV, 121ff.) where he tells how the Gothic king Filimer chased sorceresses (Lat. *magas mulieres*) into the wilderness. The Latinized Gothic word for these sorceresses is given as *haljarunae*, which reflects the purely Gothic word *\*haljarunos*. In the wilderness areas these exiled sorceresses are said to have had intercourse with "unclean spirits" who were lost in that forested region. The phrase "unclean spirits" certainly seems influenced by Christian terminology. It is further said that from this admixture the Huns were produced. This legend reflects the fact that the Huns came from beyond the forests to the east, and furthermore may explain that the Huns who did actually invade Europe were to *some* extent "Gothicized" ethnically and culturally.

The most common word for a "demon" in the Gothic Bible is *unhulþo*, a grammatically feminine word, which literally means "unfriendly one(s)". Although *unhulþo* is grammatically feminine, it is used as a masculine one time (Mat. 9.33). This translates both Greek δαιμοων and δαιμονιον. The latter term originally referred to a collective body of demons. Another term for "demon" is the grammatically neuter *skohsl* = δαιμοων. Etymologically *skohsl* means "wood-spirit" and was originally a plural form which came to be used as a singular.

It should be noted that the many biblical references to "demonic possession" seems to try the patience of the Gothic tongue. The Semites had the basic theory that diseases and maladies of all kinds (from leprosy to blindness) were caused by possession by demonic spirits. On the other hand the Germanic peoples generally believed that diseases, although they could be caused "magically" by a sorcerer, were generally and for the most part to be explained by things such as small worms, many of which were too small to be seen by the human eye. Because of this discomfort with the many "casting out of unclean spirits" found in the New Testament, Ulfilas often resorted to the Greek-derived term *daimonareis*.

## Ancestral Spirits

As strongly implied by the funerary customs of the ancient Goths, they practiced a form of ancestor worship. This was quite common among all the Indo-European peoples. The Germanic peoples often seem to have envisioned the gods as the divine progenitors of mankind, and most directly of certain ruling families, or royal dynasties.

Among the Goths there was a tradition surrounding a certain Gauts, who was both a divine hero from whom the Goths were descended, and to whose name the name of the Goths appears to have been linked. The etymon, or word element, *\*gut-* in Proto-Germanic is linked to *gaut-* by means of ablaut variation, an expected linguistic phenomenon in Germanic. Gauts is at the head of the Amali royal house to which Theodoric the Great belonged. The manuscript of Jordanes' history has the spelling as Gapt, but this is likely to have been a scribal error. Gauts is etymologically identical to ON Gautr and OE Geat, which figures prominently in the story of Beowulf.

In a famous passage in the history of the Goths by Jordanes (XII 78), he reports, following a victory of the Goths over the Romans:

> And because of the great victory they had won in this region, they thereafter called their leaders, by whose good fortune they seemed to have conquered, not mere men, but demigods, that is Ansis. Their genealogy I shall run through briefly, telling the lineage of each and the beginning and the end of this line.

This is one of the few times where Jordanes provides an original Gothic word, where he has to explain what he means in Latin. The Goths worshipped and gave thanks to what he calls in Latin *semidei*, "demigods." These are clearly ancestral spirits, the spirits of dead ancestors which make up an important part of the ancient religion of the Goths. The Gothic term *ansis*, is a later form of the more ancient spelling *\*anseis*. This word is derived from the name of the ancient ancestral gods of sovereignty and war. In Old Norse these were called the Æsir (sg. Áss), both are descended from the Proto-Germanic word *\*ansuz*, ancestral sovereign god. (In the older rune-row this is the name of the fourth rune, the a-stave, but Ulfilas did not use a variant of this for his Gothic letter ᚨ, no doubt due to its overtly pagan religious meaning.

The *anseis* are original and true gods of the Germanic and hence Gothic peoples. Some of the Gothic families thought of themselves as being descended directly form these *anseis*, but it would be a mistake to limit the importance of these entities to mere ancestral spirits. In a similar way the Vandals had their founding hero Vandill.

Closely connected to the idea of ancestor worship is the need for blood vengeance for the deaths of relatives or ancestors. Such acts of blood vengeance are very common in Gothic legend and history. (Helm pp. 20-21)

Some examples of this are when Sarus and Ammius avenge their sister Sunhilda on Ermenric (Jor. XXIV, 129), or when Gudrun/Hildico avenges her brothers on Attila. Theodoric the Great, despite being raised at the court of Byzantium was thoroughly Gothic in his morality and temperament. He avenges one relative on Rekitach, a son of Theodoric Strabo, and another relative on Odovacar, whom he is said to have killed with his own hand with the words: "I will do to you what you did to my people."

In the world the Old Norse sagas we discover more about the motivation and underlying ideology behind the idea of blood vengeance in the Germanic world. It was thought that if a relative was killed, his honor was taken from the tribe or clan. In order to restore this honor to the clan, and allow it — as a virtually concrete substance — to be reborn in to a yet-to-be-born member of the clan, a descendent, such vengeance had to take place. In Old Norse the term for avenging someone is *hefna*, which is etymologically related to our word "heave." Soul, luck, or honor of the individual had to be heaved up. lifted back into the clan of its origin. This ideology is what was at the foundation of this moral and legal imperative in the Germanic world.

## Gods and Goddesses

From the earliest times the Goths worshipped gods and goddesses in human form, just as the Greeks and Romans did. They were polytheistic, which meant that they had a variety of value centers in their complex culture. The previously mentioned *anseis* were never given up, but were allowed to "devolve" into more ancestral demigods in Christian times. In the Old Norse terminology the Æsir were contrasted with the Vanir. The Æsir were gods of sovereignty, law, magic and war. The Vanir were more gods and goddesses of the earth, of agriculture, of material well-being and riches. Although we have not myth or explanation of the contrast between the Æsir and the Vanir in Gothic lore, some scholars have been moved to indicate that the Goths were heavily involved in the worship of the Vanic deities. Helm sees this as being likely on ethnographic as well as geographical grounds. (1937, p. 34) On the other hand, a great deal of other data points to a continuing cult of the *anseis*, which was kept alive as ancestor worship, but which had its roots in the old religion. The Gothic kings of pagan and Chrsitian times would have ruled on the theoretical basis of their connection to the sacred and royal bloodline— in both instances back to the true Gothic gods— the *anseis*. One Gothic name, Ansila, which is attested from the 4th century literally means "the little god," or more clearly "the descendent of god."

Besides the word for a god derived from PGmc. *ansuz, the Goths also used the old Germanic term *guþ*, which was commonly used to translate Greek θεος, "god." Originally this term grammatically a neuter, which is remains in the compound *galiuga-guþ*, idol," in 1 Corinthians 10.19, however, elsewhere, when used to indicate the Christian god, it is grammatically masculine.

## Individual Gods

One of the oldest questions in the history of Gothic pagan theology has been whether or not the god Wodan was known to them. The name is not recorded in the sources. If it were, it would have the form *Wodans. This has disturbed many historians of religion in the past who regarded the Goths as the most archaic of the Germanic peoples and at the same time want to see the theology of Viking Age Scandinavia as essentially unchanged from Proto-Germanic times. First of all, the Goths are merely the first Germanic group to be widely attested in their own literary language. This does not make them any more archaic than any other Germanic group. Second, the Germanic theological structure, like all Indo-European pagan structures is not organized according to the names of the gods, but rather according to their functions, according to their characteristic actions.

Helm and other scholars interpret the fact that Wodans is not recorded among the Goths to mean that that god (Wōðanaz/Óðinn) was not an original Germanic god, but rather "migrated" to the north after the Goths had left. This interpretation is unnecessary. The idea of the divine pairing of Mars:Mercury = Tiwaz:Woōðanaz, which is recorded and attested by outside observers from before the Gothic migration from the north, clearly shows that a god (by whatever name) filled the function which Óðinn assumes in the Icelandic sources. Another East Germanic tribe, the Vandals, who also migrated from the north were by contrast historically connected to Wodan. So if we look at the gods of the Goths from a *functional* perspective, perhaps a clearer picture will emerge.

## Gauts

This god or ancestor, one of the *anseis*, can be taken to be the origin of the Gothic tribe, or at least of the Ostrogoths. As we have already pointed out Go. Gauts is identical with ON Gautr, which is in fact one of the many *heiti*, or bynames of the Norse god Óðinn. In ON the name seems to have something to do with being a progenitor. This is very much in keeping with Óðinn's general function as the All-Father (ON Alföðr or Alfaðir). Like Gauts, Woden appears at the head of the

Anglo-Saxon genealogies of kings. Woden and Óðinn are etymologically identical forms: the initial v- sound regularly drops off in words when it comes before a stressed vowel. This is also why we have ON Urðr, "fate," whereas the same word appears as (OHG) *wurd* or (OE) *wyrd*. Another instance which firmly connects this Gauts with the function shared by Óðinn is found in the Norse runic tradition, where we find a kenning for the a-rune (*áss*, god) the equation : *áss er aldingautr* (Old Icelandic Rune Poem, stanza 4). The phrase translates "The Ase (= Óðinn) is the ancient father." Therefore it can be said that Gauts and Wodan most likely serve some of the the same or similar functions in the respective pantheons of the Goths and North Germanic peoples.

## *Teiws

As is well-known, earlier Greek and Roman commentators established a system of name-substitutions for the gods and goddesses of other peoples. In the case of the Romans this is called the *interpetatio Romana*. Many subsequent writers in Latin adopted the same practice. In this system Germanic Wōðanaz/Óðinn was called Mercurius (Mercury) and Tiwaz/Týr was called Mars, or in Greek Αρης (Arēs). In Gothic the name of this god has been reconstructed as *Teiws. But how did the Roman god of war, Mars, come to be equated with the Germanic god of law and justice, Tiwaz? This came about because for the ancient Germanic peoples all acts of war, or any conflict of any kind, including games of chance, were conceived of as events adjudicated by the gods or by the forces of nature over which the gods may be able to exert some control. In this context Tacitus reports in the *Histories* (XIII, 57) that the Hermunduri sanctified those killed in battle (as virtual human sacrifices) to Mars and Mercury (i.e. Tiwaz and Wōðanaz).

Jordanes (V, 41) has the following to say about the god Mars:

> Now Mars has always been worshipped by the Goths with cruel rites, and captives were slain as his victims. They thought that he who is the lord of war ought to be appeased by the shedding of human blood. To him they devoted the first share of the spoil, and in his honor arms stripped from the foe were suspended from trees. And they had more than all other races a deep spirit of religion, since the worship of this god seemed to be really bestowed upon their ancestor.

This passage requires a number of additional comments. Clearly the passage refers to the same god as known among the Germanic peoples as Tiwaz. He and Mercury (Wōðanaz) were the gods who received bloody human sacrifice. Other evidence seems to show that the god of war was not so much appeased by the sacrifice of captives taken in war as he was merely receiving what had already been promised him before the battle. Archeological evidence in the north shows that the early Germanic peoples sacrificed the equipment and weapons of the defeated army (often throwing them into sacred lakes or bogs after rendering them useless by breaking or bending them), but other reports also tell of them being hung in trees, although this was probably a ritual technology more reserved to Wōðanaz/Mercury. Again Jordanes returns to the theme of the gods being the ultimate ancestors of the Goths.

The Gothic letter-name recorded as *tyz*, reconstructed by most scholars as *\*teiws*, the Gothic form of the old rune-name *\*tīwaz*, seems to reflect an old (pre-6th century) linguistic form. This can be said because after that time Gothic lost its *-s* nominative masculine singular ending (Helm 1937, p. 38)

The influence of Greek in the Gothic world is, of course, profound. This is seen in the fact that the Gothic weekday name for Tuesday (ON Týsdagr) is *\*Areinsdags*, "day of Arēs." In the Bavarian dialect this shows up as *erintac*, which among other things, is an indication of the missionary activity of the Goths outside the Gothic realms during the Migration Age.

## *Fairguneis

Helm also speculates about the presence of a thunder god who would have had the name Faírguneis, which would correspond to the Norse form Fjörgynn. This name etymologically is connected to a word for the oak, and would have translated "oak-god." This name would then have been related to the weapon the god carried (an oak club, perhaps).

## *Iggws

Scant but compelling evidence points toward the worship of a god known from common Germanic times as Ingwaz, the earth-god. Ingwaz has been identified as a Vanic deity in the north, and his name is linked with that of Freyr, whose name is really a title, "the Lord." The combination Yngvi-Freyr is known in Sweden, and Yng- may have indeed been the root of the true name of the god who went by the title the Lord (Freyr) in the north. In the Gothic realms there is evidence for the presence of this god, and further evidence that he was consciously syncretized with the new Christian cult. Ingwaz was the older rune-name for the /ng/ sound. As we see with the Gothic writing system, the /gn/ sound is spelled with a double /g/ in imitation of the Greek orthography. However, Ulfilas used the name *\*iggws* for the Greek letter X (*chi*), which was used almost exclusively in Gothic for writing the name of Christ. Ulfilas has gone well out of his way to use the name *\*iggws* and to attach it to a letter which is primarily a label for the name of the hero of the new religion.

From what we have been able to discover, we can see that the pagan Gothic pantheon was little different from the other Germanic pagan pantheons. Functionally all the major features are in place. There is a sovereign ancestral god, a god of justice and war, one of thunder and an earth-god to whom the culture was so attached he even iconically survived well into Christian times— and even among the churchmen.

## Cosmology

As no texts of an authentic pagan type survive in Gothic, the exact cosmological map believed in by the Goths remains a matter of some conjecture. However, it seems that the major features of Germanic cosmology were set in place in common Germanic times. Nothing in the Gothic material, which mainly consists of isolated words or concepts, contradicts the cosmic map as we can infer it from Norse sources, for example.

The Germanic peoples conceived of the realm of man being in the middle of the cosmos, that there was a divine realm above and a dark and misty world below. In all directions there were different qualities of being, the further out one goes on a horizontal plane. As with the Celts, the Germanic peoples often conceived of these various levels as planes, fields,or meadows.

As far as the vertical axis is concerned, surviving Gothic terminology confirms the idea that there was a higher, lower and middle realm, in the last of which humans live and thrive.

Below is the realm of the dead. In Gothic this is called *halja*, which is used to translate the Greek Ἀδης (*hadēs*). This is thought to be a misty world, but not a place of punishment. When Ulfilas is called upon to designate hell as a fiery place of punishment he feels compelled to use the foreign word *gaíaínna* (< Gk. γεεννα < Heb. *gehenna*) When translating the Greek αβυσσος (abyss) Gothic *afgrundiþa*, "the deep" is used with no apparent religious connotations, or at least no negative ones.

Above is a paradise, Gothic *waggs*, "meadow." this terminology is shared by other Germanic languages, for example Old Norse Fólkvangr, "field of the people or army," which is the abode of the goddess Freyja, Old Saxon *godes-wang*, "the meadow of god" and *heban-wang*, "the heavenly meadow" (*Heliand* 748, 2791, 5969), and Old English *neorxna-wang*— a pleasant and friendly field of the dead. This idea may also be reflected in the Gothic letter name for the w-sound (𐍅), which could either be derived from the old common Germanic name, **wunjō*, meaning "joy, pleasure," or it could be the Gothic word *winja*, meaning "meadow."

In the middle of the world is the place where humans live. In Gothic the word *midjungards* (Gk. οικουμενη) survives, meaning "the inhabited world, the world of men, etc." This Gothic word answers so perfectly to ON *miðgarðr*, OE *middangeard*, OS *middelgard*, and OHG *mittilgart*, that there can be no doubt that both the form of the word and the concept are elements inherited from common Germanic times.

As with so much else in the Gothic world the cosmology remains something which we can not be entirely sure about. However, in its broad outlines we can be sure that it reflected the general polar axis model of an upper and lower realm connected through the middle by a place inhabited by humanity, the center of the world.

## Cultic Forms

Now that we have looked at the nature of the human being, the idealized divine forms and the structure of the world according to the pagan Goths, we next want to delve into the technologies used by them in order to communicate with the higher realms of the ideal (divine) world, as well as forge solidarity and organization in this world. This latter motivation was extremely important to the ancient Goths due to the fact that they were so mobile that it was not settled landscapes, but rather social order and cohesion which gave them their sense of identity and stability in the world.

There are certain technical features of cultic activity, such as the tools or implements used, the timing of the rituals, the location of the ritual, the personalities of the active agents in the ritual, as well as the general symbolic acts performed. All of the factors combined give shape to a ritual or cultic technology the principal purpose of which is to organize and focus the spiritual life of the folk and to communicate, both actively and passively with a higher level of spiritual organization (e.g. the gods). The main act of this sort of communication is the sacrifice, i.e. the sending of gifts to the gods in exchange for what they have already given the folk or what they are bound to give them.

### Timing

Religious ceremonies or rituals are usually done at specific times. These may be on the occasion of some special event, such as victory in battle, or more usually at certain times determined more or less by natural or celestial events. For example, the popular assembly of the Goths is reported always to begin at dawn. (Apollinaris Sidonius *Carmina* VII, 452ff.) The *Lex Visigothorum Recessvindana* (VI. 2, 3) prohibits sacrificing at night to "demons." It is likely that this prohibition refers to the worship of the pagan gods, who might have on occasion originally been worshipped at night, or it may be an example of the old religion being forced into darkness and hiding.

Apparently the ancient Goths made it a part of their religious practice to perform certain rituals at the time of the full moon. This idea is obliquely referred to in Ulfilas' translation of the Bible. In Colossians 2.16 there is reference to the observation of the new moon (a Jewish religious practice), but this apparently made no sense to Ulfilas, and he replaces the idea of the new moon with one relating to the full moon (Go. *fulliþe*).

There was probably a springtime ritual circuit made by an image of a deity in a wagon pulled by animals. This appears to be the kind of rite we find reported by Tacitus (*Germania* ch. 40) concerning the goddess Nerthus, and one we hear of later in Sweden in which the image of the god Freyr is similarly caused to go about on a springtime circuit. The purpose is to bring the powerful organic blessings of the gods or goddess to the land and animals. The function of these rituals, added to the fact that in the two historical examples of a similar practice the case could be made that they are in celebration of Vanic deities further leads some scholars to point to the Vanic character of much of the Gothic cult. (Helm, 1937, pp. 59-60)

Sozomenos in his *Historia ecclesiastica* (VI, 37) reports that Athanaric sent just such a huge wagon out and commanded that any Christian who would not worship it should be put to death. This occurred in the year 348. Sozomenos tries to make it sound like Athanaric sent the wagon out with the expressed purpose of discovering Christians, when it was probably just a part of an annual ritual. The fact that the Christians would not worship the image of their community simply showed the king that he had subjects who were disloyal to the folk-group and not a part of the popular solidarity. In modern terms the refusal of the Christians was as much a "political" crime as it was a "religious" one.

In the religious technical terminology of the Goths a periodic festival, one which occurs at regular intervals of time, is called a *dulþs* "festival," while the verb *dulþjan* means "to celebrate a festival."

We know that the pagan Goths knew Yule and practiced it. The fragmentary Gothic calendar calls November *fruma Jiuleis*, i.e. the month before Yule. Also in the in the 10th century in Byzantium in December there occurred a festival which they still called the "Gothicum." This was the remnant of the old Gothic Yule-tide or Christmas celebration.

## Priests

In *De bello Gallico* (VI.21) Caesar makes the famous statement that the Germans do not have "druids" (*nam neque druides habent*). This has been interpreted as meaning that they had no professional separate class of society which has a purely religious function, as the druids were in the Celtic world. The ancient Germanic peoples certainly had priests of various kinds as the linguistic data shows and subsequent commentators and historians such as Tacitus describe priestly functions.

Gothic terminology provides several words for "priest," all of which are derived from the pagan terminology. Most frequently used is *gudja* which translates Greek 'ιερευς (*hiereus*). This is an ancient Germanic term, and is even found in one early fifth century runic inscription. This is the stone of Nordhuglo (Krause 1966, pp. 146-147) discovered in western Norway. The text of this stone reads:

ᛖᚲᚷᚢᛞᛃᚨᚢᚾᚷᚨᚾᛞᛁᛉᛁᚺ///
ekgudjaungandiRih///
*ek gudja ungandiR ih ///*
I (am) the priest, unaffected by sorcery *ih ///*

Here we have an ancient term for "priest," etymologically linked to the word for "god," PGmc. *guð*, "god." *Gudja* becomes *goði* in Old Norse. Additionally, this inscription shows a term for magic or sorcery, *gandiR*, ON *gandr*, the negative *un-* prefix probably indicates that the priest is immune to the effects of sorcery or knows how to counteract it. The symbol /// indicates that the stone is broken off at that point.

Two other terms for "priest" occur in the gospel of John. One is *weiha*, priest. It comes up in the phrase *auhumists weiha*, "high(est) priest" (John 18.13) and translates the Greek term 'αρχιερευς (*archiereus*). Originally the term *weiha*, derived from PGmc. *wīhaz*, holy, inviolate, sacred" must have indicated the priestly function of making objects, space, time, etc., separate from the mundane or profane world. This originally contrasted with another word for "holy," *hailagaz*. The latter term indicated something that was holy due to its being filled with divine power. This dichotomy of the holy has been much discussed in Germanic culture. For a summary of this question, see "The Holy," by Thorsson printed in *Green Rûna* (Rûna-Raven, 1996). Most Germanic languages did not preserve both terms for the holy equally. As a result of the Christianization process the nomenclature of the holy was simplified, as was the case for most religious concepts, and one or the other of the terms fell into disuse.

The third term for a priest which seems derived from pagan nomenclature is *gudblostreis*, which means "divine sacrificer" and is used to translate Greek θεοσεβης (*theosebēs*), "worshipper of God" (J. 9.31). The Gothic word is a compound made up of the well known element *gud-*, "god," and *blostreis*, "sacrificer." The latter element is related to Old Norse *blót*, "sacrifice."

It is likely that Ulfilas is not shy about using pagan terminology to describe the priestly functions of the Jews in the Bible because the historical and cultural contrast Jews : Christians was used by early churchmen to draw a distinction between indigenous pagans and Christians. Therefore old pagan terminology could be used to describe the activities of the Jews while a newer, more internationalist terminology was used to describe Christian activities and functions. This attitude perhaps also often led the Jews into friendly relations with pagans, Arians and other non-Roman Catholic and non-Orthodox peoples.

Helm (1937, p. 48) identified the Naharvali as an East Germanic tribe and cites the report of Tacitus (*Germania* ch. 43) that the priests of the twin-gods, the Alci, regularly don the dress of a woman in order to cary out their rites. Another example of the peculiar dress of the Gothic priesthood arises when we analyze the appellation given to the Gothic priests who are called the *pillaeti*, which means those "wearing a *pilleus*." A pilleus is a felt cap made to fit close to the head like half an egg. (Helm 1937, pp. 48-49) This may have arisen as a result of a confusion with Getae, an Irianian tribe, or it may have been a fashion taken over by the Goths from Iranian Getae.

As concerns the organization of the Gothic priesthood, it is obvious that it is not very hierarchical. Every social unit at every level had its own independent person functioning in priestly role— the family, clan, tribe, and nation. The king seems to have been the priest for the whole nation. This is further enforced by Eunapius (*Fragm.* 55) who reports that every φυλη, "clan" brought its own priests and sacred objects with them north of the Danube when they crossed it around 376. Among the Burgundians Ammianus Marcellinus (28, 5, 14) reports that the most powerful of their priests is called Sinistus "the oldest." Ulfilas uses the title *sinista* for πρυσβυτερος (*prysbyteros*). So it would seem that the Arian church organization was more informal and looser than the Roman Church, following the lead of the pagan Gothic culture. Eunapius also mentions priestesses 'ιερειας (*hiereias*)— but they were probably actually *seeresses*, according to Helm (1937, p. 51).

## Pagan Ritual Elements

No document exists which describes what a Gothic pagan ceremony or ritual would have looked like. There are, however, copious references to various ritual features in historical descriptions, and linguistic data also give us a great deal of insight into the rituals of the pagan Goths and the theories which lay behind them.

### Sacrifice

The usual words for "sacrifice" with Ulfilas are *saljan* or *gasaljan* which indicate the idea "to bring forth, transfer." This fits well with the basic theoretical idea that the process of "sacrificing" was one of making something sacred, giving it over to the world of the gods The sacrificial object or victim is made separate and inviolate, i.e. *weihs* and made holy *hailags*. *Hailags* seems to have been avoided by Ulfilas, perhaps because of its pagan connotations. (Helm 1937, p. 53; 57)

Other terms are revealing about the background of pagan Gothic ritual. The word *sauþs* means "sacrifice, offering" and translated the Greek θυσια (*thysia*). Etymologically it means "the boiling (of meat)," and is derived from the verb meaning "to boil." This word can be compared to the Old Norse word for "sheep," *sauðr*. Another Gothic word frequently used to translate Greek θυσια is *hunsl*. This is a widely attested word in Germanic for "sacrifice." We also find Old English *hûsel*, "the eucharist" and Old Norse *húsl*: "housel." Although this is attested almost entirely only in a Christian context, the word is Germanic and not borrowed from Greek or Latin. Its etymology is also controversial. The fact that it occurs as a Gothic verb, *hunsljan*, "to sacrifice," (Gk. σπενδειν) and in a compound Gothic *hunslastaþs*, "place of sacrifice, altar" makes it likely that it was a Gothic word which was borrowed into the other languages at an early date. It probably originally referred to the substance of the sacrificial meal, i.e. the meat of the victim which was consumed by the folk. This was then naturally and easily transferred to the "Corpus Domini." Ulfilas also uses *blotan* in a pure Christian sense of "worship" (Helm 1937, p 55-6) However, the term is also one that was inherited from pre-Christian religious terminology, its cognate is found in Old Norse *blóta*, "to worship (with sacrifice)," Old English *blôtan*, "to sacrifice" and Old High German *blozan*, "to worship." The plain Germanic verb "to give" and the noun derived from it, Gothic *giba*, "gift, giving" was also used in a sacred or holy context to mean "sacrifice." This noun seems to have been the name of the Gothic *g*-letter.

Another conspicuous element of Gothic religious ritual is the circumambulation of a divine image, which nevertheless was not practiced in all cults. This circling of a central symbolic object was also a part of funerary rites with the mourners doing this on horseback around the burial mound (Jordanes IL, 257) This was probably an Indo-European feature from the steppe culture. It has been noted that the Huns also did this, but in the Germanic rites this was done is a solemn way, whereas among the Huns is was a wild affair. That this mode of mourning was a part of the most ancient Germanic funerary ritual among the heroic class is evidenced by the final passage in the Old English *Beowulf* where we find a detailed description of the ceremonial of the cremation of the hero which includes twelve chieftains riding around the grave mound signing songs praising the hero and lamenting his loss. (*Beowulf* 3171ff.)

Other features include *laiks*, "dance," which probably originally related to measured movements used in sacrificial actions. This term is also found in Old English *lâc* "sacrifice." There was also song and oath-taking. (Helm 1937, p. 53) Singing of some sort seems to have been important to the pagan Goths and it continued to be a conspicuous part of holy services even in Christian times.

Oath-taking plays a large part in Gothic history. For example it is recorded that Athanaric swears an oath to his father never to step foot on Roman soil (Ammianus Marcellinus 27, 5, 9). This same Gothic king also swears an oath of peace with the Emperor Valens (in the Fall of 368). The Visigoths swear an oath before the battle of Salices (377). This was probably an oath of renewed loyalty. Helm notes that in history, after Christianization of the Goths, oaths were most usually broken. However, these oaths were generally sworn to non-Goths. This clearly demonstrates that among themselves the oaths were inviolable, but as far as enemies or non-Goths were concerned, they could be used duplicitously. The story of St. Sabas shows family members protecting Christian Goths — and even swearing false oaths to fellow Goths to protect them. This demonstrates an example of blood-ties superseding "religious" ones, or "legal" ones. In reality all three types of relationships reflect deep cultural features. (Helm 1937, pp. 64-65)

In heroic literature the famous example of the fight between the father and son, Hildebrant and Hadubrant, in which obligations of oath took precedence over blood-ties forms a mythic icon.

Around 600 the East Germanic Gepids are reported to have had a nocturnal festival involving ritualized drinking. This was probably a heathen practice which was later transferred to some saint (Helm 1937, pp. 59). A funerary feast was held at the mound of the dead. In Gothic this feast was known as a *straua*. "funerary feast." This term is derived from the Gothic verb *straujan*, "to spread, strew" which referred to the laying out of the corpse and grave goods in state. Feasts were similarly held at the grave mounds in remembrance of the dead at Yule-tide (Helm 1937, 20).

As already discussed the Goths had various forms of sacrifice. Things which were sacrificed in this process ranged from valuables to animals (which were consumed in a form of sacral meal) and human beings. In the last case the victims of sacrifice were usually prisoners (criminals or prisoners of war) or slaves.

Votive offerings of valuables were common. The famous deposit Pietroassa is likely an example of this kind of sacrifice. Most of these deposits come from the second to fourth centuries. At least thirty of these were known by the early 20th century, although most of such deposits would have been discovered and looted in antiquity, of course.

That the animal sacrifice was both essentially a religious affair and a communal meal is shown in the *Martyrdom of Sabas* which reports that Christians were forced to eat sacrificial meat.

Human sacrifice was practiced as a part of funerary rites, when sometimes prisoners and slaves were sacrificed and burned along with the the bodies of noblemen. Isidor of Seville, writing in the *Chroicon Gothorum* (14) reports about Radagais that in 405 when he attacked Italy he declared that if he won the battle the blood of all the Christians would be considered a sacrifice. This can be directly compared to the attitudes reported by Tacitus concerning the Hermunduri who similarly considered all enemy combatants killed in battle to be tantamount to human sacrifices to the gods. (Helm 1937, p. 55-6.) The Vandal king Gelimer has captured citizens killed in honor of his fallen brother, Ammatas (Procopius *De bello Vandalico* I,20).

Among the Goths human sacrifices were usually bloody ones (to the war god), but also sacrifice by drowning was known. The aforementioned Christian St. Sabas was so drowned in 372. This martyrdom is mentioned elsewhere, but otherwise in the literature concerning the prosecution of Christians by the Goths this type of "martyrdom" is not mentioned. (Helm 1937, p. 56.)

Drowning the victim of sacrifice is akin to the general cult practice of sacrificing objects in water. Bog finds from late imperial times along the Baltic (between the Oder and the Passarge) indicate that coins, amber and glass beads, bronze objects, necklaces, etc., were so sacrificed. These finds have led some to compare the practice to the worship of Nerthus (Tacitus *Germania* ch. 40). Among these finds no objects relating to men (weapons, etc.) are found. Helm points to this form of human sacrifice and the procession with a divine image as indicative of specifically Vanic practice among the Goths. He additionally points to the apparent Christian equation between *Iggws, a Vanic Earth-God, and Jesus as an indication of the Vanic character of early Gothic religion. (1937, pp. 41-2). The more likely interpretation, given what we can see of the fully developed ancient Gothic pantheon, is that Jesus, as a Man, i.e. a human being who has been perfected, is equated with the Earth-god simply because he became a god on earth.

Several ritual elements are reported that are particular to funerary rites, e.g. that there is a solemn procession with the corpse, accompanied by a clashing of weapons, there are songs in honor and praise of his deeds and of lament (Jordanes XLI, 214). The solemn procession on foot is a common Indo-European feature. The Gothic word for a song of lament is *gaunoþus*, "lament for the dead." Funerary songs of lament are specifically Gothic and specifically opposed by the Roman church. In Article 22 of the Acts of the Synod of Toledo (589], which concluded with the transition of the Goths from Arianism to Roman Catholicism, it is specifically indicated that the people are to sing Psalms at funerals— not the *carmen funebre* which the folk had been singing previously. (Helm 1937, pp. 18-19) Finally the particular practice of riding around the grave mound on horseback in a ritual circumambulation must again be cited as a peculiar Gothic practice (Jordanes IL, 257).

## Shrines

Helm (1937, p. 45) mentions a variety of types of sacred sites used by the Goths, e.g. groves (*trunci*), holy lakes and mobile shrines or temples on wheels. Ambrosius (*Epistola* 20,12) says of the Goths that their wagons are not only their homes, but their churches as well. As this is not a usual Christian practice it is most likely that this stems back to heathen practice and custom.

There is an old Gothic word, *alhs*, which means "sanctuary." It is used by Ulfilas to translate the Greek ναος, "temple" and 'ιεπον, "holy area." Etymologically this term is derived from Proto-Germanic *\*alhaz*, all Germanic attestations of which indicate that it was a temple, grove or holy enclosure. We also have Old English *ealh*, "temple." All of this evidence does not exclude the idea that the *alhs* did not contain a building or structure of some kind (Helm 1937, pp. 45-6).

Another term used by Ulfilas to translate Greek 'ιεπον (*hieron*), is *gudhūs*, "god-house." This compound word seems to suggest specifically a temple building. This appears to be a word invented by Ulfilas, and it occurs only once in John 18.20. Although permanent large structures for religious worship are not definitely attested, it does appear likely that some sort of structure was part of the sanctuary complex, or the *alhs*.

## Holy Objects

Because the record of Gothic culture is so much represented by the idea of treasures and mysterious artifacts, certain objects possessing some sort of holy or sacred quality, such treasures have always played a part in the process of rediscovering the secrets of the Goths. Certain items appear to have been necessary for the performance of many rites of the pre-Christian Gothic cult, for example a wagon, animals (either for people to ride or to pull the wagon), and divine images to be transported in the wagon (Helm 1937, p. 47). There is a description by Flavius Vopiscus in *Vita Aureliani* which indicates that a Gothic wagon was actually pulled by a deer (Helm 1937, p. 60-1). This can be compared to the fact that among the Scythians ceremonial costumes for horses were fashioned which made the horses appear as if they were deer or stags. (Rice 1957, plate 11)

## Spears

Both written and archeological sources demonstrate the importance of the spear to the symbolic practices of the early Goths, and Germanic tribes generally. I will address this subject in much more detail in chapter 5. At this point it suffices to say that spears, such as those discovered at Kovel and Dahmsdorf, were obviously ceremonial objects. They were never used in combat, and were decorated with symbols of religious meaning and tribal affiliations. The ritual and symbolic uses of spears in Germanic culture are well documented and extremely archaic. Tacitus notes that the young man, when he comes of age, is invested with a shield and spear by his father (*Germania* ch. 13). The spear is seen as a legal symbol and one of sovereign power. (Jan de Vries 1956-57, II, 13-14)

## Rings

One of the most spectacular examples of Gothic religious symbology is represented by the now fragmentary ring of Pietroassa. The details on this particular ring are more fully discussed in chapter 4. It is known that the earliest reported symbol of Germanic kingship is not the *crown* but the *neck ring*, and it appears that this is what the ring of Pietroassa actually is. Its original function is a matter for further discussion, however, it appears that the treasure of which it was a part was not a hidden "temple treasure," but rather a votive offering or sacrifice (Helm 1937, p. 47).

Rings are an important part of the symbolic temple equipment reported from the Viking Age. The oath or altar ring is mentioned in several accounts in the Icelandic literature (de Vries 1956-57, I, 390). The best single description is that found in chapter 4 of the *Eyrbyggja saga*. This account lists objects such as a solid ring weighing twenty ounces, upon which the people swore oaths. It is further said that the priest wore the ring on his arm at public meetings. Here we are reminded of a letter written by bishop Ambrosius of Milan in the year 381, which mentions the fact that the Gothic Arian priests wore such arm-rings and that the bishop condemns this practice as a heathen one.

## Kettles

The use of symbolic vessels, especially cauldrons or kettles by the Goths also appears to have had a special importance. Such vessels were an indispensable part of the semi-nomadic life-style led by the Goths for many centuries. The steppe peoples in general were known for their vessels of this kind. In Norse mythic literature there is a famous account of a kettle found in the Hymiskviða in the *Poetic Edda*. This kettle is necessary for the brewing of the mead for a religious feast. The myth contained in this poem has been compared to an Indian myth about the god's acquisition of the divine *amṛita* (de Vries 1956-57, II, 132). This would perhaps be of some help in explaining the importance of the Gothic letter name for the hʋ-sound, *\*hʋaír*, "kettle" (𐍈).

# Magic and Divination

Magic and divination are classic categories to be investigated. However, the categories were probably not as neatly separated out from the rest of religion, or from each other, in pre-Christian times. The distinction appears to be a largely political or social one, between pre-establishment and antiestablishment activities which either promote the general welfare and solidarity of the folk, or which detract from general well-being or lead to the disintegration of the folk. In other words, the king, chieftains and heads of families may have conducted rites using the same technologies and methods used by what would be called "witches." The difference was in the perceived aims of the rites— either constructive or destruvtive toward the welfare of the culture.

## Magic

Magic is the use of symbolic communication in order to operate within reality, either to cause things to change which usually would not change, or to prevent or preserve from change those things which would ordinarily change. Traditionally magic is marked by its occasional, rather than regular, daily, or seasonal use.

There is no Gothic word recorded for "magic" or "sorcery" *per se*. This is for the most part due to the fact that the passages of the Bible which might have given us these terms have not survived.

Female necromancers — those who were able to call upon the spirits of the dead in order to elicit information — were called *haljarunos*. This term appears to be a common Germanic one, since it also occurs in Old English *hellerune* and Old High German *helliruna* both also indicating a sorceress.

The story of Filimer's distrust of the sorceresses known as the *haljarunos* (Jordanes XXIV, 121ff.) is reflected many centuries later in the Norse Hávamál (stanza 155), where we read about Óðinn, god of magic and kings, advising rune-magicians about how to combat practitioners of malevolent sorcery.

Gothic laws such as the *Lex Visigothorum Recessvindana* and the *Leges Burgundionum*, written in Latin and from Roman times, nevertheless testify to the general belief in the malificent acts of witches to harm human health and crops. It must always be assumed that when there are laws against something, it is something which is either practiced by people, or something of which the population has a concrete fear. These nefarious acts include the preparation of magical drinks (*venena*), the tying of knots (*ligamenta*) designed to harm people or plants. In the case of the harm done to people by these magical knots, there is specific mention of the idea that such sorcery could rob men of their voice. There is also specific mention of the opening of graves and desecrating them (*L.V.R.* XI, 2,2). This activity was probably undertaken by sorcerers to obtain certain body parts for use in specific magical spells. In these same laws there are some reports of *incantationes* for causing bad weather, and the use of *invocatio*, the calling on demons, either in voice or in writing, to make men lose their right senses (Helm 1937, pp. 26-8).

## Divination

Typically in the Germanic world divination, that is the obtaining of information from the divine world, or from the fabric of the world itself, took place in three types of operations. One is the direct accessing of the world of the spirits or demigods by a seeress. This is a direct, but subjective operation. This may have been part of the repertoire of the *haljarunos*, as the etymology of the word would seem to suggest this. Another two types of operations fall under a more objective category. These are the observation of signs or omens in the world and the casting of lots (perhaps with the aid of runes).

The taking of omens is indicated by the Gothic word *taikns*, "sign, wonder" which translates Greek σημειον (*sēmeion*) This Germanic root is found in other Germanic languages with similar meanings, e.g. (OE *tâcn*, and OHG *zeihhan*). It also seems to have been borrowed into Finnish in Proto-Germanic times as *taika* (Helm 1937, p. 29). Biblical references to a wondrous sign, Greek τεπας or σημειον are translated by Gothic *fauratani*, which literally means a foretelling sign. An example of this in pagan times would be the account concerning the Vandals in which an eagle is seen as a bird that provides certain "signs" (Procopius *De bello Vandalico* I,4). Concerning the casting of lots, Jordanes reports (LVI, 283) that the Goths cast lots to determine whether or not to go to war.

## Myths and Legends

No myths or legends of the Goths themselves survive in their own language. But their fame and reputation was so great that other Germanic peoples recorded many such legends relating to the Goths. Most of these belong to the heroic cycle of myth as well as to the genre of legends attached to historical figures such as Theordoric the Great.

Some scholars of the early part of the century were of the belief that the Goths were responsible for everything great in the Germanic culture due to their early contact with the Greeks. These scholars thought, for example, that Eddic mythology was of Gothic origin. There is no hard evidence of this, so such a theory must be doubted. Likewise the theory that the Goths were the inventors of the runes based on Greek models must be abandoned. The runes date from before any Gothic migration to the area near the Greeks. However, it is not unlikely that elements of the runic tradition might have been influenced by the Goths, as it is certainly true that 1) the Goths had great prestige in the North and 2) there was regular and ongoing contact between the Goths and their original homeland in Scandinavia and the Baltic region.

In Germanic heroic mythology there are two great cycles of tales, known as the Nibelungen-Cycle and the Dietrich-Cycle. Epic and poetic literature connected with these cycles survive in Old Norse, Old High German, Middle High German and Old English. Both of these cycles of literature are connected to legendary material which often has ties to the history of East Germanic tribes— especially the Burgundians and the Goths.

The Burgundians were the tribe into which the (Cheruskan?) Sigurd came and which was attacked by the Huns along the Rhine in 436 CE. The latter part of the Nibelungen story is a legendary account of the interactions between the Burgundians and Huns. Literary works which relate to this cycle include the Middle High German *Niebelungenlied* and *Klage*, the Old Norse *Völsunga saga*, and various other works in Old Norse and early modern German.

On the other hand, the Dietrich of the second cycle of legends reflects the German form of the name otherwise recorded as Þiðrekr or Theordoric, and is mythic account of the heroes at the court of Theodoric the Great in his Ostrogothic Kingdom. Literary sources which relate to this cycle include the Old Norse *Þiðreks saga af Bern*, the Old High German *Hildebrantslied*, and several other works. For a convenient survey of this literature see Edward R. Haymes' *Heroic Legends of the North* (Garland, 1996). It should be noted that the *Þiðreks saga af Bern*, although surviving only in Old Norse (having been complied in Norway around 1200 CE), is actually a translation of an older Old Low German text, which has disappeared.

Gothic culture was significantly influenced by the cultures it encountered in from the Russian steppe to the Balkans. It should be remembered, however, that the influence of some of these non-Germanic peoples on Germanic culture goes right back to the time when the Germanic peoples were first differentiating themselves from other Indo-European groups in northern Europe. The Northern Iranian horse-cultures, the Scythians and Sarmatians, interacted with the Germanic (as well as Slavic and to a lesser extent Celtic) peoples of central and eastern Europe from as early as 700 BCE. The symbiosis between and among these peoples led to confusion on the part of classical authors as to the identity of certain groups. Goths were often confused with "Scythians," and the other way around.

As far as the lasting effects of pre-Christian religion on Gothic culture in general, Helm (1937, p. 64) cites the following:
1) Respect for and attention to omens and signs
2) Deep feeling of ancestral bond and tribal solidarity
3) Importance of the oath (Go. *aiþs*) and swearing (*sweran*) and swearing falsely *ufarswaran* — with the invocation of fate and an ensuing harsh form of self-cursing in those cases when oaths were broken.

In summary it can be said that the substance of pre-Christian Gothic tradition— their religion and other aspects of their ideological culture differed very little from the other Germanic tribes. Most apparent differences are probably the result of defective or sparse source material. What was unique about the Goths was their extreme sense of identity and group solidarity in the face of hostile surroundings and their ability to succeed in an extraordinary way over several centuries while maintaining their identity and solidarity. It should also be noted that the Goths seem to have had a certain genius for interacting productively with non-Germanic peoples— especially the Northern Iranian peoples. Of the Migration Age Germanic tribes, it is the Goths and the Franks and the Anglo-Saxons who succeeded best while having migrated far outside what had been age-old Germanic territories or areas immediately adjacent to them. The Anglo-Saxons succeeded because they moved into a power vacuum— southern Britain was abandoned by the Romans and the Saxons, Angles and Jutes moved in. The Franks succeeded by making an alliance with Rome and the Roman Christians against the other Germanic tribes. But the Goths moved into the very heart of the old empire, challenged it in its own heartland, and were victorious. It is this level of historically heroic success coupled with the strong Gothic sense of identity (aided by its peculiar religion) which made the Goths the stuff of enduring legend. It is now time to turn our attention more pointedly to the mysteries of the Gothic Church itself.

# Gothic Christianity

### Christianization of the Goths

From their first contact with the Romans some Goths interacted positively with them and some became Christians when they crossed into the Empire. But early on they remained a small minority and were mostly limited to commoners and slaves as well as the descendants of slaves or captives.

The most important figure in the early history of Christianity among the Germanic peoples is Ulfilas (311-383). His name is also recorded in

Greek as Ουλφιλας. His mother was a Cappadocian captured by the Goths in a raid into the Empire in 214, his father was a Goth. He was raised as a Christian among the Visigoths and went to Constantinople to study Christian doctrine. At that time Christian teachings were dominated by the Arian version of theology and Christology then supported by the Emperor Constantius II. The Arian doctrine itself is named after Arius of Alexandria, who lived in the early part of the 4th century CE. The Arian doctrine mainly contradicted that of the Roman Catholic teachings concerning the dogmas surrounding the Trinity— that God was *One* "in Three persons." In other words God was one and three at the same time, without in any way compromising his unity. In contrast to the latter, Arianism stated that the Father came before the Son, the Son (logically!) emanated from the Father and that the Holy Spirit was a third term in a triad of divinity. This doctrine was officially declared a heresy in the church following the Council of Nicea (325), but the doctrine lived on sporadically in the East for many decades. In any event, most experts on the religions of the early Christian Goths agree that the form of Christianity practiced by the Goths was not even true Arianism, but rather it had to be an essentially Gothic form of religion and a sort of syncretism between Christian and non-Christian elements in Gothic culture.

Ulfilas was made bishop in 341 and undertook a mission among the Gothic peoples as well as other ancient Germanic folk. By 395 most of the Visigothic realm could be characterized as at least nominally Christian. The genius behind Ulfilas' mission was his translation of the Christian Bible into vernacular Gothic, the apparent use of popular tunes set to Christian words in the liturgy (also performed in Gothic), and the preservation of other Germanic elements in the Gothic church. We will review all of this in somewhat more detail later. The Arian doctrine itself provided the theoretical or doctrinal distinction between the Germanic and Roman cultures which was necessary for the Goths to be able to embrace Christianity at all. At first this was effective, but over time it would prove to be the political downfall of the Goths.

As a result of the mission of Ulfilas, the Ostrogoths were nominally Christianized (between 405 and 450). Earlier, the other major East Germanic tribes, the Vandals and Burgundians, were also nominally converted to Arianism just before 400 CE. Other southern Germanic tribes were also affected by the Gothic mission, e.g. the Alemanni, Bavarians and Thuringians, but it cannot be said they were actually Christianized at that time.

Among the Goths themselves this mission was sometimes met with hostile opposition. Between 368 and 372 the Visigothic king Athanaric tried to drive Christianity — both Roman and Arian — out of his kingdom. Christianity was opposed on two grounds: 1) it was feared that it would destroy folk-solidarity and 2) it was seen as "Roman religion" and the Goths generally remained suspicious of things Roman. But the Gothic Christian movement was to a large extent successful due to the characteristics instituted by Ulfilas. The religion of the Goths was clearly neither orthodox Christianity, nor doctrinally bound to Arianism. Although on a superficial level they ceased adhering to traditional Germanic religion, it was essential that they maintain their cultural independence from the Romans. They did this by retaining many features of their native traditions.

## Tenets of the Gothic Church

Specific beliefs which separated the Goths from other Christians are difficult to rediscover. There must have been many, since the religion of the Goths was so despised by the Roman Catholics. Chief among these differences was the previously mentioned Arian teaching contradicting the dogma of the Trinity. Biblically the doctrine of Arius is well-supported by the clear statement in John 14.28, when the Son actually says: "I am going to the Father, because the Father is greater than I am." Arianism is further supported by logic and philosophical consistency. The Orthodox position only had the advantage of appearing to solve the problem of "polytheism." The Goths simply continued being polytheists— maintaining a plurality of religious value centers and not persecuting their fellow religionists for having different beliefs and practices from themselves.

Ulfilas left behind a personal *Credo* which was recorded shortly before his death by a certain Auxentius. It reads:

> I believe there to be only one God, uncreated and invisible. And (I believe) in his only begotten Son, our Lord and God, the architect and fashioner of all creatures, to whom there is no one who is similar, Therefore there is one God, the Father, who is the God of our God.

This document may at first appear confusing. Is there one god or two? The answer seems to be there are at least two named here. The "one God" (Lat. *unus Deus*) is tantamount to the Platonic or Neo-Platonic concept of the One, the Good, the Light, etc. This entity is the *Absolutum*. This is the God of another God, called the Son— who is clearly cast in the role of the demiurge, the God who fashions all of creation as an intermediary between the Absolute and creation itself. The Absolute, or the Good, or the Light is the God of the Son. The Good is absolute and transcendent. The Son is Creative. The Holy Spirit is the Plan of Creation, the World-Soul.

The tenets of the ancient Gothic Church partook of not only Christian elements, but also of pagan Greek philosophy and pre-

Christian Germanic tradition. The inner teachings of the church can be understood from a thorough understanding of all the subjective elements we have discovered in this study. Some also insist on the idea that the Gothic Church has survived underground to this day. Upon this idea the current Gothic Church of God is founded.

It is likely that the secret teaching of the Gothic church was that Jesus was not co-eternal with God, that God was an abstract principle, and that the Son was a heroic god-man, who became God-like as a result of two things: 1) his noble [semi-divine] ancestry and 2) his own *heroic* efforts. The function of the church was to further this teaching and continue the tradition founded by the Lord among the Goths. Jesus may or may not have died on the cross— it is more likely that the Goths taught that he survived the ordeal, as Wodans/Gauts might have done, and continued his line of divine ancestry elsewhere.

## Ritual of the Gothic Church

The ritual or liturgy of a church is a complex thing. It includes how time is arranged for ritual, the space in which the ritual is conducted, as well as the actual form of the actions and words performed during the rite. Only a few fragments of this information remains to us today. The records of the Gothic Church were largely destroyed by the Roman Catholics over the years.

We know fairly little of the Gothic religious calendar. A fragment of a calendar survives on one leaf of manuscript (Milan, Ambrosiana Codex p. 36 sup. + Turnin Theca F IV 1, Frag X). This fragment covers 23 October to 30 November. November is also called *fruma jiuleis*, fore-yule, in Gothic. This shows a survival of pagan terminology, as Yule is a common Germanic term for the festival which occurred around the winter solstice. We know nothing of the Gothic Church's attitude toward Yule itself, other than the name was still used after the Goths had been nominally Christianized. "Christmas" was not observed by the early Christian church at all. It was only with Germanic influence that this time of year required special celebratory activity. The Gothic calendar shows memorial days not only for well-known early Christian saints, but also for specifically Gothic martyrs to persecution and for the Emperor Constintius II, who had been a friend of the Goths. It should also be noted that the Gothic Church observed the sabbath on Saturday, hence the Old High German weekday name *sabaztac* ("sabbath-day"), which found its way into areas of Germany where the Gothic missionary activity was felt. This is also why one finds *Samstag* for Saturday in southern Germany even today, whereas in the north *Sonnabend* is heard.

# Gothic Ritual

In the early church — of all sects — the central activity was that of the liturgy of the holy mass. In orthodox term this was a ritual which in symbolic terms reenacted the sacrifice of Jesus — the Son and Lord (Go. *Frauja*). The central magical act was one in which the body and blood of the Savior was symbolically reproduced in bread and wine and these talismanic substances were then ingested by the faithful, thus making the substance of the Lord and that of themselves closer together, and thus bringing them closer to salvation.

The liturgy itself is the whole set of words and actions which the priest — a man consecrated to do this work — must perform in order that the rite be effected. We know a good deal about the actual Gothic liturgy. This is because fragments of it have survived, as well as the fact that the over all form of the rite was not substantially different from the rite performed in the 4th century in Thrace, from where the liturgy was first taken. It is essentially the Greek rite of Constantinople, *mostly translated into the Gothic language.*

This last point is of tremendous importance because it was most usual in the ancient world for peoples other than Greek or Latin speakers to have to content themselves with hearing the entire rite in a tongue foreign to their own. This included the "sermon" or the homily portion of the rite. Although the people may have understood only their own language, the priests would still "sermonize" to them in Greek or Latin. One of the revolutionary breakthroughs of Ulfilas is that he used the language of the people— not only to translate the Bible, but also in the ritual.

It had also been disdainfully said of the followers of Arius of Alexandria, who had committed his teachings to lyric poems collected in a volume entitled *Thalia* — songs of joy — that they set his words to sailors' songs and those of millers. There is no evidence that the Gothic Arians did the same thing, but they did use their own language instead of an "international koiné." There is additional abundant evidence that the Goths did continue to preserve their own heroic national (pagan) songs— not as part of the Eucharistic rite, of course, but as the substance of other ceremonies important to the spiritual lives of the people.

In ancient times one of the most important parts of the mass was when the people chanted "lord have mercy!" — Greek κυριε ελησον! — which in Gothic was *Frauja armai*! Gothic warriors sometimes used this as a battle-cry as they charged into the fray.

At one point in the rite also, the people were to recite the so-called Lord's Prayer. In Gothic this is:

*Atta unsar þu in himinam, weihnái namō þein. qimái þiudinassus þeins. waírþái wilja þeins, swē in himina jah ana aírþái. hláif unsarana þana sinteinan gif uns himma daga. jah aflēt uns þatei skulans sijáima, swaswē jah weis aflētam þáim skulam unsaráim. jah ni briggáis uns in fráistubnjái, ak láusei af þamma ubilin.*

To this was also added the formula:
*Untē þeina is þiudandardi jah mahts jah wultus in áiwins. amēn.*

It should be noted that the word "father" is not the expected *fadar*, but rather the more colloquial *atta*, "pappa" or "daddy." This is also the Gothic word upon which the name of the Hunnic king Attila — "little daddy" — is based. While in other places the Lord's Prayer, or Pater Noster, was to be recited in Latin, a mysterious language to most, here it is recited in the people's own language. This prayer was generally thought to have magical or operative powers. Throughout medieval magic the use of this text is a fairly universal formula for invoking or expressing magical powers.

## Ancient Gothic Church Structures

The liturgy is the central activity of the church. The place created for this activity to take place is the church building. The earliest Christians paid little attention to church structures, as they generally met in remote open areas, grave yards and catacombs. The first buildings fashioned exclusively as meeting places were not based on Greek or Roman sacred architectures, as might have been expected, but rather on secular buildings. The wealthy Roman generally had a large all-purpose room in his villa for banquets and so on. This became the basis for most church structures. In the Hellenic east there were some examples of centralized structures and this was often used as the model for Gothic churches.

Only a few examples of Gothic church buildings survive, and none in exactly the form the Goths had them built. Most of them differ very little from structures built for the orthodox sects— whether eastern or western. This is because the artisans who built these early (pre-711 CE) structures were not Goths, and because leaders such as Theodoric the Great wanted to emphasize outward conformity of the Goths to *Romanitas*. But there are some Gothic features worth mentioning.

In Ravenna the best example of Gothic church architecture is the building now called S. Apolinare Nuovo. It was built and consecrated by Theodoric the Great in 504 as his palace church. Originally it was dedicated to the Savior, Jesus Christ. It seems that the Goths, despite their theological position concerning the absolute divinity of Jesus, were far more dedicated to his person than were the orthodox Romans.

This is perhaps because they saw him in the role of the divine hero, or even divine ancestor, whom they were used to worshipping. This church still preserves much of the magnificent mosaic work on its walls that Theodoric had commissioned. The altar was placed in the middle of the basilica by the Goths— not at the far east end of it as the Romans did. On the right, or southern, wall is the image of the enthroned Jesus surrounded by angels. On the opposite wall is the image of Mary and the baby Jesus. The three Magi approach to honor Jesus. It is thought that the Goths had the Magi so placed to emphasize the idea that it was Jesus, and not Mary, who was being honored. As the liturgy was performed, the women would be on one side facing the image of Mary and the baby Jesus, and the men would be on the other, facing the enthroned Jesus. Other original mosaics depicting Gothic martyrs were destroyed after the Goths were ousted and the church was reconsecrated as a Roman Catholic church. Some of the surviving mosaics were also altered. Originally Jesus was shown holding a book, upon which was inscribed: *Ego sum rex gloriae*, "I am the king of glory." This was changed to show him holding a vessel of holy oil or water.

Other church buildings of the Goths in Ravenna, e.g. the Church of the Resurrection and the Church of St. Andreas (Andrew) were substantially destroyed. The Gothic baptistry remains as does the previously mentioned Tomb of Theodoric. Although the latter structure could be discussed as a holy edifice, it appears clear that its sanctity stems from the ancient court culture of the kings, and not from that of the church.

Other surviving church buildings constructed by or for the Goths in Spain and France include San Pedro de Nave, Santa Cristina de Lena, San Miguel de Escalada, Santa Columba in Bauda (northwestern Spain) and the chapel of Germigny-des-Prés. The Visigothic structures show distinctive traits of the style brought to the west from the east. Remnants of similar structures have been found on the Crimean Peninsula, where some Goths survived until the 16th century. There has also been some speculation concerning the possible influence of these structures on the stave churches of Scandinavia. However, this similarity of structures — a central design rather than a long hall-like one — could also be explained as an inheritance from the North. Then it would simply be that the Gothic churches and the stave churches both derive from the same pre-Christian northern design principles.

### The Gothic Bible

The entire Bible was translated by Bishop Ulfilas, or under his supervision, in the 4th century. Only fragments of this translation survive in various manuscripts. Most of what remains is from the New Testament and comes from the magnificent manuscript called the Codex Argenteus— the "silver codex." It is called this because the letters are written with a silver ink on parchment which has been dyed purple. Initials and other features also are written with gold ink. Early sources written by Philostorgius and Sozomen suggest that Ulfilas did not translate the Book of Kings because of its "warlike" nature, and Ulfilas was trying to tone down this bellicose tendency among his fellow tribesmen.

This Bible was not prepared to be read directly by lay persons (such as Luther's Bible of 1534). It was for the education of the Gothic priesthood and for the various readings in the liturgy, which, as we have seen, was performed *in Gothic*. This allowed the Gothic parishioners to hear the biblical material in their own language on a regular basis. This set the average Gothic believer apart from other Christians in western Europe who heard the mass only in Latin— a language which only the clerics could understand clearly.

In order to write the text, Ulflias invented a new alphabet. This writing system is examined in detail in chapter 3.

The Codex Argenteus is in itself a great cultural treasure. It is now housed in the University Library in Uppsala, Sweden. Only 187 of its original 336 leaves survive. The codex was prepared in northern Italy, probably for Theodoric the Great. At some point it was taken to the monastery of Monte Cassino, whence it was taken by Liudger, a pupil of Alcuin, who founded a new monastery at Werden near Cologne, Germany, in the late 8th century. It is interesting to speculate on just why this manuscript was taken north of the Alps at that time. The codex remained in the monastery at Werden where it was subsequently "discovered" by humanists working in the 16th century. For examples, J. Goropius Becansus published the "Lord's Prayer" from the codex in 1569. It is noted that by the beginning of the 17th century the manuscript had become quite mangled. The Emperor Rudolf II had the codex brought to Prague, and in 1648 it was sent to Queen Christine of Sweden by Count Königsmarck as a gift. It was bound in silver in 1665, but the designation Codex Argeneus already appears in 1597, so the name refers to the silver letters and not to the silver binding.

The Gothic Bible and the script in which it was written were obviously of extreme cultural importance to the Goths. Perhaps there are secrets concealed in this data, which, if decoded, can yield new information about the esoteric teachings of the Goths.

Chapter Three

# Mysteries of the Gothic Alphabet
## and the Gothic Cabbala

One of the greatest mysteries and cultural treasures of the Goths is encoded in its unique alphabet. The Gothic alphabet is emblematic of the intellectual and spiritual Gothic synthesis of Germanic and Greco-Roman cultures. We know historically that this alphabet was invented by Ulfilas as an aid in completing his translation of the Bible. Clearly on several levels this system synthesized elements from the common Germanic writing system known as the runes and the Greek and Roman letters— perhaps with the customary dash of inspired innovation.

In order to understand the Gothic alphabet thoroughly, we must review what we know of the runic tradition at the time of Ulfilas. The runes constituted an early Germanic writing system which seems to have been directly inspired by the Roman script. However, the ancient Germanic peoples did not slavishly follow the Roman model, but rather innovated an entirely new system suited to their own cultural needs. The runes may go back to as early as 150 BCE, as the oldest possible runic inscriptions, the brooch of Meldorf, dates from the middle of the first century of the common era and, as a general rule of alphabetic development, the date of the actual origin of a system usually antedates the first attestation by between one hundred and two hundred years.

The Germanic *fuþark* — so called because the first six sounds of the runes were f, u, þ, a, r, and k — at the time of Ulfilas appeared:

Table 3.1: The Older *Fuþark* (150 BCE–800 CE)

| f | u | þ | a | r | k | g | w |
|---|---|---|---|---|---|---|---|
| h | n | i | j | ei | p | z | s |
| t | b | e | m | l | ng | d | o |

This system indicates certain peculiarities of the fuþark. It did not follow the usual ABC or ABG order of the Mediterranean scripts. It was divided into three groups of eight, later called *ættir* ("families" in Old Norse). It shows a clear formal relationship to the Roman capital letters as far as the shapes of many individual runes is concerned, ᚠ/F,

69

R̆/R, H/H, etc. However, it also shows clear signs of autochthonous innovation, ᚦ/th, ᚠ/w, ᛉ/j, ᛏ/z, °/ng, etc. It should be noted that the innovated signs generally stand for sounds not found in Latin or which were not recognized by the Romans as independent sounds or phonemes.

In addition, later tradition indicates that the runes bore distinctive *names* which had definite meanings in Germanic. Table 3.2 shows these names in their reconstructed Proto-Germanic forms. This is the language which would have been the common ancestor to all of the Germanic dialects.

Table 3.2: Names of the Older Runes

| Number | Shape | Phonetic Value | Name | Meaning of Name |
|---|---|---|---|---|
| 1 | ᚠ | f | *fehu* | livestock, wealth |
| 2 | ᚢ | u | *ūruz* | aurochs |
| 3 | ᚦ | þ | *þurisaz* | giant (thurs) |
| 4 | ᚨ | a | *ansuz* | a god |
| 5 | ᚱ | r | *raidō* | riding, wagon |
| 6 | ᚲ | k | *kaunaz/kēnaz* | sore, ulcer/torch |
| 7 | ᚷ | g | *gebō* | gift |
| 8 | ᚹ | w | *wunjo* | joy |
| 9 | ᚺ | h | *hagalaz* | hail |
| 10 | ᚾ | n | *nauþiz* | need, distress |
| 11 | ᛁ | i | *isa* | ice |
| 12 | ᛃ | j | *jēra* | good year, harvest |
| 13 | ᛇ | ei | *eihwaz* | yew |
| 14 | ᛈ | p | *perðrō* | peach-tree (?) |
| 15 | ᛉ | z | *elhaz* | elk |
| 16 | ᛋ | s | *sowilō* | the sun |
| 17 | ᛏ | t | *tīwaz* | sky-god |
| 18 | ᛒ | b | *berkanō* | birch-twig/goddess |
| 19 | ᛖ | e | *ehwaz* | horse |
| 20 | ᛗ | m | *mannaz* | man, human being |
| 21 | ᛚ | l | *laguz* | water |
| 22 | ᛜ | ng | *ingwaz* | earth-god |
| 23 | ᛞ | d | *dagaz* | day |
| 24 | ᛟ | o | *ōðila* | ancestral property |

Ulfilas knew this runic system. His knowledge is demonstrated by his use of runic material in his invention of the Gothic alphabet. By inventing a set of sound-sign symbols Ulfilas was following in the mythic track of other culture-heroes, and even gods, of the past. By creating an alphabet he could teach a philosophy in ways deeper than any who would come after him who were obliged to use his system of writing. To write is to create, but to create the alphabet with which others write is the consummate creative act in culture.

We know very little *directly* about the runes as they were used in the Germanic world at the time of Ulfilas and before. Fewer than twenty-five inscriptions have survived from the lifetime of Ulfilas and before. These are spread out all over northern and eastern Europe. Almost all of these are on small, moveable objects such as brooches and weapons. The most remarkable of these that seem directly connected to the Goths are discussed in chapters 4 and 5.

The runes held a sacred place in early Germanic culture. The word *rūnō* means "mystery." For example, when Ulfilas translated the passage in Luke 8.10: "Unto you it is given to know the mysteries of the kingdom of God," he did so in Gothic as follows: *izwis atgiban ist kunnan runos þiudisassaus gudis*. The Gothic word for "mystery" is *runa*. When Ulfilas translated the Greek words for letters (of the alphabet), for which there were two, στοιχιον and γραμμα, he used the Gothic words *stafs* (pl. *stabeis*) and *boka*, respectively. In Germanic these words were also closely connected to the word for "rune." For example, in Old High German we find the word *buohstap*, modern German *Buchstabe* for a letter of the alphabet, while in Old Norse the use of the term *stafr* as an alternate for *rún* is well-known.

To understand how Ulfilas understood these words, we can look at the Greek terms he was translating. Obviously the word runa, by which he translates the Greek μυστηριον, refers to the secret, hidden, or unknown meaning that lies behind the obvious or "literal" meaning of anything— including a letter of the alphabet. Greek στοιχιον is the usual word used by the Greeks for a letter of the alphabet. Its meaning in Greek is "element." It is the same word used to denote the universal elements (στοιχεια) fire, air, earth and water, for example. For this Ulfilas uses *stabeis*, staves, i.e. "elements." Finally, the Germanic word boka was used to indicate the physical appearance of the letter— in Greek a γραμμα.

This terminology revels a shared attitude between the Greeks and Goths along with other rune-using Germanic peoples, as regards the process of writing and reading. It was for them a sacred thing. Our modern sensibilities, often numbed to the presence of actual mystery and holiness, usually fail to recognize this truth today.

The Germanic runes were a sacred script, Ulfilas was familiar with them in Gothic culture. The Greeks at this time also had a sacral — if often philosophized — attitude toward the alphabet. In this cultural mix, Ulfilas could not help but have been shaped by these attitudes and himself imbued his writing system with a similar holy quality and essence.

# The Gothic Alphabet

The alphabetic system which, according to church historians Sozomenos and Philostorgius, was created by Ulfilas appears in table 3.3 below. It was used to write the Gothic translation of the Bible made by Ulfilas, but went beyond this to be used in subsequent, now mostly lost, Gothic texts.

Table 3.3: The Gothic Alphabet

| 𐌰 | 𐌱 | 𐌲 | 𐌳 | 𐌴 | 𐌵 | 𐌶 | 𐌷 | 𐌸 |
|---|---|---|---|---|---|---|---|---|
| 1 | 2 | 3 | 4 | 5 | 6 | 7 | 8 | 9 |
| a | b | g | d | e | q | z | h | þ |

| 𐌹 | 𐌺 | 𐌻 | 𐌼 | 𐌽 | 𐌾 | 𐌿 | 𐍀 | 𐍁 |
|---|---|---|---|---|---|---|---|---|
| 10 | 20 | 30 | 40 | 50 | 60 | 70 | 80 | 90 |
| i | k | l | m | n | j | u | p | — |

| 𐍂 | 𐍃 | 𐍄 | 𐍅 | 𐍆 | 𐍇 | 𐍈 | 𐍉 | 𐍊 |
|---|---|---|---|---|---|---|---|---|
| 100 | 200 | 300 | 400 | 500 | 600 | 700 | 800 | 900 |
| r | s | t | w | f | ch | hv | o | — |

As can be seen from the table, the Gothic system accounted for sounds as well as numbers. In this it followed Greek tradition, seen in table 3.4. When Greek letters were meant to be used as numbers, they were followed by a diacritical mark, e.g. $\alpha' = 1$. Similarly, a Gothic letter, when contained within points, e.g. ·𐌰· = 1, indicates a number and not a sound. However, the fact that sounds and numbers were both represented with the same system leads to the natural symbolic conclusion that numbers can be sounds, and sounds numbers on an esoteric level.

As far as the origins of the individual Gothic letters are concerned, the majority are clearly based on Greek letter-shapes, e.g. 𐌰 ← A, 𐌱 ← B, 𐌲 ← Γ, 𐌳 ← δ. However, a few are based on Roman letters: 𐌷 ← h, 𐍂 ← R, 𐍃 ← S. While some appear derived from old Germanic runes, e.g. 𐌸 ← ᚦ, 𐌾 ← ᛃ, 𐍀 ← ᛈ, 𐍆 ← ᚠ, 𐍉 ← ᛟ. Also the numeral sign for 900 is the same as the ancient t-rune (↑), which stood for the god *Teiws (ON Týr). ·T· = 300, ↑ = 3x300 = 900 .

Table 3.4: The Greek Alphabet

| α A | β B | γ Γ | δ Δ | ε E | ϝ | ζ Z | η H | θ Θ |
|---|---|---|---|---|---|---|---|---|
| 1 | 2 | 3 | 4 | 5 | 6 | 7 | 8 | 9 |
| a | b | g | d | e |  | z | ē | th |

| ι I | κ K | λ Λ | μ M | ν N | ξ Ξ | ο O | π Π | ϟ |
|---|---|---|---|---|---|---|---|---|
| 10 | 20 | 30 | 40 | 50 | 60 | 70 | 80 | 90 |
| i | k | l | m | n | j | o | p | — |

| ρ P | σ Σ | τ T | υ Y | φ Φ | χ X | ψ Ψ | ω Ω | ϡ |
|---|---|---|---|---|---|---|---|---|
| 100 | 200 | 300 | 400 | 500 | 600 | 700 | 800 | 900 |
| r | s | t | y | ph | ch | ps | o | — |

The admixture of these three cultural monuments, i.e. the three different writing systems — Greek, Roman and runic — tells us something about the spiritual and cultural matrix of Ulfilas' ideas in general. It was a mixture of Germanic (Gothic), Greek and Roman. In this, however, the Greek probably took the dominant conscious role, with Roman material taking a secondary place. The native Gothic substratum, however, must have taken a dominant subcultural and unconscious role.

The Greek alphabetic characters have names, but these are merely sound-formulas based on the Semitic names of the letters, e.g. *alpha* ← *alef*, *beta* ← *beth*, *gamma* ← *gimel*. From a 9th or 10th century manuscript, called the Salzburg-Vienna Alcuin-manuscript, there is a record of the *names* of the Gothic letters— amazingly these reflect for the most part the names of the ancient Germanic *runes*. As this manuscript dates from several centuries after the disappearance of the Gothic language in the west, it is somewhat of a mystery as to how they came to be recorded. This manuscript could have been derived from an older one, which came in the Austrian region from either the Visigothic territory of southern France, or from formerly Ostrogothic Italy.

A complete chart of the Gothic system of numbers, sounds, letter-shapes, names and meanings of the names, appears in table 3.5. It will be noted that the form of the names recorded from the Salzburg-Vienna codex often appear mangled. This is perhaps to be expected in a manuscript written at a time so far removed from the time when Gothic was actually being spoken, and living informants, if they still existed, must have been scarce. The odd spellings are generally explicable in terms of old English and Old High German scribal practices, and since English and German scribes were largely responsible for collecting these manuscripts at the time, this is to be expected.

## Table 3.5: The System of the Gothic Alphabet

| I<br>No. | II<br>Sound | III<br>Shape | IV<br>Name | V<br>Normalized Name | VI<br>Translation of Name |
|---|---|---|---|---|---|
| 1 | a | 𐌰 | aza | *ahsa | axel |
| 2 | b | B | bercna | *baírkan | birch-twig |
| 3 | g | Γ | geuua | giba | gift |
| 4 | d | 𐌳 | daaz | dags | day |
| 5 | e | є | eyz | *aíhʋs | horse |
| 6 | q(u) | u | quertra | *qaírþra | bait/bore hole |
| 7 | z | Z | ezec | *aiz | metal, coin |
| 8 | h | h | haal | *hagl | hail |
| 9 | þ | ψ | thyth | þiuþ | the good |
| 10 | i | Ι ï | iiz | *eis | ice |
| 20 | k | K | chozma | *kusma | sore |
| 30 | l | λ | laaz | *lagus | water |
| 40 | m | Μ | manna | manna | man, human |
| 50 | n | N | noicz | *nauþs | need |
| 60 | j | G | gaar | jer | year |
| 70 | u | Π | uraz | *ūrus | aurochs |
| 80 | p | Π | pertra | *paírþra | pear-tree (?) |
| 90 | — | Ч | — | — | — |
| 100 | r | K | reda | *raida | wagon |
| 200 | s | S | sugil | sauil | sun |
| 300 | t | T | tyz | *teiws | god |
| 400 | w | Y | uuinne | *winja/wunja | meadow/joy |
| 500 | f | F | fe | faíhu | riches |
| 600 | x (ch) | X | enguz | *iggws | a man |
| 700 | hʋ | Θ | uuaer | *hʋaír | kettle |
| 800 | o | Ω | utal | *oþal | ancestral property |
| 900 | — | ↑ | — | — | — |

The first column of table 3.5 indicates the numerical value of the letter, the second shows the shape of the Gothic letter and the third column indicates the basic phonetic value of conventional transcription of the letter into the Roman alphabet. The fourth column shows the letter-name as recorded in the Salzburg-Vienna manuscript, while the fifth records the Gothic word corresponding to the name either as the word appears in attested texts, or as the word has been linguistically reconstructed. Reconstructed forms are preceded by an asterisk. The last column is a translation of the name.

It is likely, given the contemporaneous learned Greek attitudes toward sound, number and meaning that the fact that the Gothic system provides for a clear and meaningful correspondence between these three categories — sound-number-meaning — that this symbolic opportunity to extract mysterious meanings hermeneutically would not have gone unexploited by the originator or subsequent users of this system. Additionally, such attitudes might have been re-imported into the rune-using culture of the north after the 4th century from this Gothic source.

It should also be noted that Ulfilas must have had a reason for inventing a new system of writing for recording the Gothic language. Gothic could have been written in Greek letters or Roman ones. Either of these two options would have brought the Goths inevitably closer to the Imperial world and the mainstream of Christendom. Therefore it can only be that Ulfilas, from the beginning, and for whatever underlying reason, wanted to create a national (Gothic) tradition. In this he seems to have rejected the basic internationalist and universalistic mission of the church as found in the Greco-Roman world. His mission seems to have been an more mysterious one, even from the beginning.

Certain past attempts to explain the esoteric meanings of the Gothic letters have been rather shallow. It is an obvious error to assume that for the Goths using these letters, the signs were thought of merely as substitutes concealing the ancient rune-lore of the pre-Christian Goths. To do so is to ignore the obvious contribution of Hellenistic lore connected to the *stoicheia* ("elements/letters") of the Greek alphabet. While the names appear to be largely Gothic (Germanic) in origin, the numerical system is primarily Greek. Both have a bearing on the esoteric quality of the Gothic letter.

Before discussing the esoteric meanings of the Gothic letters it should be noted that some of them appear to be intentional re-namings, i.e. *ahsa, "axle" for *ansuz, "ancestral god"; þiuþ, "the good" for þurisaz, "giant"; and ezec (?) apparently for *elhaz, "elk." Krause (1968, p. 66) notes that Old Norse elgr, "elk" is used as a byname for Odin (~ Wodans). These would then all appear to be examples of the Christian Ulifas avoiding what were obviously pagan "religious" references. It is curious to note in this vein that he does not seem to have avoided the use of *teiws, which might mean that this word had been revalorized with Christian connotations, although it is not used in the extant portions of the translation of the Gothic Bible. Even more remarkable is the apparent "Christianizing" of the name *iggws (← *ingwaz), which originally meant "the Earth-God," and in the system of Ulfilas seems to have been made to stand for Jesus Christ himself.

## The Esoteric Meanings of the Gothic Letters

### 𐌰 1 A

The reconstructed Gothic letter-name, *ahsa, indicates an axle or axis— a shaft or pole which turns, and around which something, such as a wheel or the vault of heaven, turns. This concept was important all the way back to Indo-European times and the migratory Goths, who often lived in wagons, understood the hidden meaning of the concept very well. The older, pagan, name was ansus— ancestral sovereign god. This god is the source of the people and their support. Old Norse áss (the corresponding Norse rune-name) could also mean the main roof beam of a house. The One is the source of all things and the support of all. *Ahsa is the One, which is both everything and nothing at once.

### B 2 B

*Baírkan, birch-twig, is the letter denoting the concept of nature, the dyad which follows the monad of 1. As the birch was a traditional instrument not only of judicial chastisement, but also an instrument used to raise the natural forces of fecundity— both through flagellation — it can be seen that this the perfect complex symbol of nature in all her guises. The dyad is Nature in motion and dynamic growth.

As a side note this letter can have nothing to do with the bear esoterically. The word "bear" is a euphemism (meaning "brown-one") and is not related to the hidden name of the bear— which would have been related to the Latin ursus, e.g. the Old Norse proper name Yrsa, "she-bear."

### Γ 3 Γ

Giba is the same word as found in the old rune-name. However, for the Arian Goths it had definite connotations of a divine or spiritual gift which endowed the recipient with spiritual powers or abilities. These can be the gifts of the Holy Spirit, the third person in the triad, Father, Son, and Holy Spirit. For the Arians, who maintained the logical relationship among these three "persons," the third was the provider of knowledge (γνωσις, kunþi) and the mean between all extremes.

## ᛞ 4 Δ

"Day" is the meaning of the fourth Gothic letter. Its quadratic symbolism is further reinforced by the old runic shape ᛞ. The Old English Rune Poem states that "day is a sending of the lord, dear to men, glorious light of the creator, mirth and hope to the prosperous and to the poor, of benefit to all." This indicates that the concept was one of universal benefit to all men. In the Greek numerical lore of the time it was considered the key of nature and the "nature of change."

## ᛖ 5 E

The name of this letter, *aihvs*, means "horse." The Goths became expert horsemen. They learned their skills on the steppe from the Scythians and Sarmatians. The association between the Goths and horses was so strong that the word *goti* in Old Norse could even mean "a horse." In Greek number-lore the pentad is associated with the manifestation of justice and marriage, and it is called "the immortal." In Germanic lore the horse is seen as symbolic of the power which carries the soul from one level of being to the next.

## U 6 —

The manuscript form of the name *quertra* has been reconstructed as *qaírþra*, which some have defined as "bait" (Krause 1968), others as a technical term for the bore-hole in which a fire-producing vertical stick is placed. (Schneider 1956, pp. 142-7) The hexad in Greek symbolic arithmetic indicates the form of forms, order, reconciliation, health and perfection. It is tempting to see fire symbolism in this letter, as the sixth rune in the *fuþark* is *kēnaz*, "torch."

## Ƶ 7 Z

Of all the letter-names this is the most problematic. The manuscript could be read *ezec* or *ezet*. This is difficult to reconstruct as a Gothic word. It seems likely that the first part of the word corresponds to Gothic *\*aiza*, "copper," "bronze" or "brass." It occurs in the words *aiz*, "coin" and *aizasmiþa*, "coppersmith." The seven is the heptad, which carried the meaning of fortune and due measure (Gk. καιρος).

77

## ᚺ 8 —

The manuscript name *haal* demonstrates the influenced of an English scribe, who might have palatalized the *-g-* in **haal*, as in OE *hægl* [hail]. The old meaning of this name was that of catastrophe, but it also could mean "cosmic order." This reflected the Pythagorean concepts connected to the octad, both "untimely born" and "harmony."

## ᚹ 9 Θ

The name of this letter reflects the Gothic word *þiuþ*, meaning "the good," or "the good thing." Greek philosophy teaches that the Good, the Agathon (Gk. αγαθον) is the ultimate abstract power or "thing" from which all and everything else is derived. The fact that *þiuþ* is an abstract, mathematical concept is further demonstrated by its ninth position in the system and the fact that the signs for 90 and 900 are not letters but purely abstract mathematical symbols. But note too that the abstract symbol for 900 is ↑ the old rune-shape for the word "god" (**teiws*).

## ᛁ 10 Ι

The number 10 is a bridge to the next level of numbers and letters. The Old Norwegian Rune Poem calls "ice" a "bridge" (over water). While the Old English Rune Poem emphasizes the jewel-like beauty and perfection of the substance of ice. 10 links or bridges the unity of 1 in a vertical fashion to a more manifest reality.

## ᚲ 20 Κ

The number 20 is the phenomenon resulting from the dyadic principle. The sore or wound results from flagellation by the birch. Clearly the manuscript name, *chozma*, is related to the Old Norse rune-name *kaun*, "sore, wound." This is the experience of transformation, the real-life feeling of undergoing profound change.

## ᛚ 30 Λ

**Lagus* can be called "water," but it refers to fluid or moisture in general. The ordinary word for "water" is *wato*. This is the triad on a more phenomenological level. The gift, God's grace, is transferred to the phenomenon of fluidity — wine — and made absorbable by man.

## ᛘ 40 M

*Manna*, which translates Greek ανθροπος, refers to human beings in general, or as a class of beings. This is the common mass of humanity which inhabits this world of *midjungards*. This Gothic cosmological term, which answers perfectly to Old Norse miðgarðr, is used to translate Greek οικουμενη, "the inhabited world," or "the earthly orb." Here we have the more manifest dimension of the tetrad.

## ᚾ 50 N

The Gothic word *naups* translates Greek αναγκη (*anankē*), meaning "necessity" or "compulsion." This is an important word and concept in Greek magical thought of Late Antiquity. It is the force of compulsion exerted by a superior being on an inferior one. This is the phenomenon behind the pentad.

## Ϩ 60 —

Gothic *jer* does not directly correspond to a Greek letter, but as the number 60 it is the manifestation of the hexad. Its Gothic name means "year," but it is used to translate a number of Greek words, e.g. 'ενιαυτος, "a cycle or period of time," καιρος, "exact or critical time," χρονς, "a long time" (Luke 20:9), and 'ετος, "a year." This is a cycle punctuated with critical moments.

## ᚢ 70 O

The Gothic letter ᚢ bears the name *\*ūrus*, "aurochs," but corresponds structurally to the short Greek o, *omikron*. The *ūrus* was a fierce, wild bovine creature akin to our bison and longhorn. This creature roamed only in the north, and would have been unfamiliar to the Greek world. As the phenomenon of the heptad, it would have corresponded to the idea of being "hard to subdue."

## ᛈ 80 Π

For structural reasons the old rune-name *\*perþrō* can be said to have probably denoted a pear-tree, or the wood from a pear (fruit-bearing) tree. The reconstructed Gothic letter name *\*paírþra* was rooted in this symbolism, although the meaning of the name in Gothic is now obscure. Linguistically it can have nothing to do with Greek *pithos*, "pot," as the -r- remains unaccounted for phonologically.

## ᚱ 100 P

The Gothic letter-name here clearly corresponds to the old rune-name *raiðō*. *Raida* means wagon, a vehicle used by the Goths in their centuries-long history of migration. The migratory Goths lived in their wagons and they even had temples and later churches transported within wagons.

## S 200 Σ

*Sauïl* is the sun, which translates Greek ἡλιος (*hēlios*). In Gothic the word, normally of feminine gender grammatically and mythologically, is treated as a neuter noun. This may have been a philosophical statement regarding the transcendent nature of the sun as a philosophical and religious concept rather than a simple physical phenomenon.

## T 300 T

The old rune-name *teiws* is retained here. Although it is not recorded as a word for "god" in the Gothic Bible, it must have nevertheless been understood as a universal name of god, corresponding to Greek θεος (*theos*) and Latin *deus*. As a word and name it would then have also included the old Gothic god(s) in this universal category of divinity.

## Y 400 Y

In the Salzburg-Vienna codex the name is given as *uuinne*. This shows the Old High German spelling practice of writing a double-u for the [w]-sound. The old rune-name was *wunjō*, "joy." But the manuscript name does not directly reflect this. Rather it seems to refer to the Gothic word *winja*, "pasture" or "meadow"— which would have been understood perhaps as a heavenly plane. If, however, the old name applied, it would be reconstructed as *wunja*, "joy."

## ᚠ 500 Φ

The Gothic word *faíhu* translates Greek αργυριον, "money" (Mark 14.11), κτηματα, "possessions" (Mark 10.22), and χρηματα, "riches" (Luke 18.24). To the Goths this concept related directly to the importance of Gothic *treasures*— gold and mobile wealth hidden or stored away for later *higher* use.

## 𐍇 600 X

This Gothic letter is unique. Its shape is that of the ancient g-rune (*gebō*, "gift"), the concept of which is accounted for in the third Gothic letter. The phonetic value of the Gothic letter is that of the aspirated Greek letter χ, the first letter in the title Christ (Gk. Χριστος). In the Gothic Bible it is practically used only in the spelling of this word, which is usually abbreviated 𐍇𐍃. What is unique is that the name of the Gothic letter is *enguz* in the manuscript— reconstructed as **iggws* [ingus], clearly a reflection of the ancient rune-name **ingwaz* (OE Ing), "the earth-god." So here we have the clear indication that the name of a *pagan* god has been used to interpret, and give deeper meaning to, the "Christian" god. This at once tells us something of the Gothic conception of their particular Christ, their Christology, and their understanding of the importance of Iggws. This is esoteric evidence that Christ/Iggws was considered *a* divinity, but one who was terrestrial, or immanent, in nature, not entirely transcendent.

## 𐍈 700 Ψ

Of course, there is no phonetic correspondence between Gothic 𐍈 (hʋ) and the Greek Ψ (ps). They do, however, bear the same numerical value. The Gothic letter shape could be construed as the shape of Ψ viewed from above, if the "bowl" of Ψ is seen in three dimensions. This would also give us insight into how letters could be envisioned in ancient times. The Gothic letter-name **hʋaír*, reconstructed from *uuaer*, means "kettle" or "cauldron." This may have no runic correspondence, and thus may have been "invented" by Ulfilas. In these times, however, pure invention out of whole cloth, especially for a man steeped in tradition, seems unlikely. Coupling this idea with the fact that the concept of **hʋaír* has no overt Christian meaning or correspondence leads us to believe that the name reflects an older, alternate runic tradition. The Proto-Germanic name would have been **hweraz*, "kettle, pot, cauldron," which might have been an alternate name for the h-rune. Such kettles were of great importance for the domestic life of the ancient Germanic peoples, and even more important to those who regularly migrated across long distances, such as the Goths.

## 𐍉 800 Ω

Here there is a perfect correspondence between the Gothic letter-name and the rune-name, and between that and the Greek sound (long-o). The concept of "ancestral property" took on a more abstract meaning for the frequently migrating Goths. *Oþal is clearly transferred to institutions and interpersonal relationships which then can be projected onto any landscape the people possessing these offices happen to be occupying at the moment. This secret of maintaining a high level of social organization and group solidarity while being constantly on the move is an old Indo-European one, but one the Goths practiced very effectively.

---

All of these letters indeed remain *runes* in the sense that they reveal and conceal meanings far in excess of their simple phonetic values and that each is part of a larger symbolic context or matrix of meaning. In the case of the Gothic world, however, it is a great and fatal mistake to assume that the system is restricted to being a crude mask of the older runic system. The Gothic set of letter-symbols represents a true synthesis of the Greek and Germanic worlds.

## The Gothic Cabala

### Numerology

The Greeks introduced the idea of using letters as numbers to the Semitic world. Early manuscripts of the Hebrew Bible used Greek letters as numbers in enumerating the chapters and verses of the texts. Originally — in Homeric times — the Greek system used letters to signify the numbers 1-24 only. Somewhat later a system of three rows of nine symbols was developed. This was structurally identical to the system shown in table 3.4 above. Using this system higher numbers could easily be written. As the Greeks called their "letters" στοιχεια, "elements" it is clear from early on that the saw that, as Pythagoras was to remark, "number is the foundation of all things." This included language and its "elements."

By the time the Goths encountered the Greek world in the 2nd century, the Greeks had already developed an elaborate and sophisticated numerological philosophy and esotericism. This was pioneered at the earliest stages by philosophers such as Pythagoras, who lived around 500 BCE. This Greek form of esotericism was absorbed by the Hebrews and became a mainstay of their esoteric tradition known as the *kabbalah*, "tradition." Because the Jews were so well able to transmit this type of material from ancient times right up to the present day, this sort of esotericism is now often referred to generically by the Hebrew name Kabbalah.

When Ulfilas created his system of Gothic letters he would have had available to himself not only ancient pagan Greek esotericism, but also a vast, by that time heavily Christianized, body of lore surrounding the letters and numbers represented by the Greek system of the στοιχεια. What we have in the Gothic system is a unique synthesis, not a simple transference of older runic ideas and not a slavish imitation of a Greek model. The mysteries of this system are vast and can only be touched on in this volume.

In theory the esoteric meaning of the elements of the system hinges on the hidden link between the three factors of number-sound-shape. Perhaps the relationships among these factors were colored by theology. For example, the orthodox Romans might have insisted on the essential unity or identity of these factors, while the Gothic "Arian" (and pagan Greek) approach might have seen it more as number giving rise to sound, which is then expressed in visible form.

On one level the Gothic system is a matrix of symbolic meaning on its own. It can be studied and meditated upon in ways which reveal deeper significance derived from the interplay of the factors of number (order), sound (name) and shape (form). One example of this emerges from the Late Antique and early Christian focus on the "triple numbers," 111, 222, 333, etc. This is perhaps most famously known about in connection with the "number of the Beast" (666) recorded in Revelation 13.18. (Note there is an alternate textual tradition which makes the number of the Beast 616.) What is often missed in connection with these triple numbers is that they are really formulas relating to the three letters in each of the *vertical columns* in the system shown in table 3.3. For example, Gothic •𐍂𐌹𐌰• is $100 + 10 + 1 = 111$.

Moreover, the Gothic system provides for the possibility of deriving esoteric meaning beyond that of the Greek system simply because the names of the letters invite meaningful semantic speculation which the abstract Greek letter names do not allow. In meditating on this system it should be noted that the numerical reading proceeds from the bottom up:

1

↑

10

↑

100

On the other hand the semantic reading, *and* the more esoteric numerological understanding proceeds from the top downward:

1
↓
10
↓
100

The latter simply demonstrates the fundamental ancient idea that the numbers 1-9 are root *qualities* from which any and all subsequent numbers are derived. The numbers 1-9 constitute true archetypes of meaning; they are the fathers from whom the other numbers descend and upon whom others are dependent.

Using these principles as our foundation the following meditations emerge:

|  | Archetype | Phenomenon | Epiphany |
|---|---|---|---|
| 111 = ᛅᛁᚴ = | *ahsa* (1) | *eis* (10) | *raida* (100) |
|  | axel | ice | wagon |

The turning or supporting pole of the universe provides the principle for traveling a solid, yet slippery (dangerous) surface (bridge) which is collectively achieved in a vehicle or wagon. The wagon equipped with axles for its rotating wheels crosses the ice.

222 = **BKS** = *baírkan* (2)   *kusma* (20)   *sauil* (200)
　　　　　　　birch-twig　　sore　　　　sun

The birch-twig is the instrument of chastisement and stimulation for change and growth or discipline which inevitably causes pain (and results in a sore or wound) but which ultimately results in the experience of a transcendent and nurturing spirit.

333 = ᚷᛚᛏ = *giba* (3)   *lagus* (30)   *teiws* (300)
　　　　　　gift　　　water　　　　god

The gift from an archetypal level is that of consciousness or the spirit, conveyed to mankind in the ritual form of the ingestion of consecrated liquids. In pagan times this was mead (honey-wine) or beer/ale, while in Christian times it was seen as the consecrated wine of the eucharist. This leads to the presence of god in the world.

444 = ᛆᚼᛦ = *dags* (4)   *manna* (40)   *winja* (400)
           day          human         meadow

Day-light is that which shines on all and everyone. The four-fold symbol describes the place of human existence. The light of day distinguishes humanity and rightly seen can fashion a happy existence for the whole— in this world and beyond.

555 = ᛂᚾᚠ = *aíhʋs* (5)   *naups* (50)   *faíhu* (500)
           horse         need          mobile property

The horse is the power of the "other," the greater archetypal power that completes and expands man's power. In times of necessity, distress or war this phenomenon of power provides for man winning manifest and tangible power in the form of goods and gold (treasure). This treasury, wisely dispensed, was also an instrument of alleviating distress. For the often warlike Goths the horse was an instrument necessary for their prosperity gained through conflict.

666 = ᚢᚸᛪ = *qaírþra* (6)   *jer* (60)   *iggws* (600)
           fire             year        Man

The fire, or instrument for making a friction-fire where no fire existed before the instrument was used, is ceremonially ignited at certain times of the year— especially in the spring when a new fire is ignited. This cyclical fire, brought from heaven to earth, inaugurates the higher Man— ᛪᚱᛁᛋᛏᚾᛋ.

777 = ᛎᚾᚩ = *aiz* (7)   *urus* (70)   *hʋaír* (700)
           metal       aurochs       kettle

Metal is the archetypal substance which is so hard it requires a hot fire and great strength to extract it and to forge it into a useful object in the world, e.g. the kettle or cauldron. This in turn becomes an essential tool for the transformation of organic materials into higher substances, e.g. in cooking or brewing.

888 = ᚺᚠᛩ = *hagl* (8)   *paírþra* (80)   *oþal* (800)
           hail         pear            ancestral property

Hail is the symbol of great archetypal catastrophe raining down from above— it is the catalyst for sudden *change*. The "fruit bearing tree" provides knowledge, γνωσις, by which change can be understood and harnessed. This allows for the possibility of the development of permanence in the sea of change. The ancestral property is a stable inner force in the individual and group which provides a sense of permanence amidst constant outer turmoil.

999 = 𐍈𐌿𐍄 = *þiuþ* (9)   90        900
              the Good    90        900

This triad of "letters" is unique in that only one, the 9, has a phonetic value. The other two are purely abstract numbers with no additional names. All this points to two things: the ennead is unique and the Good is the highest element. The Good (Gk. Αγαθον) is abstract and beyond all personifications or anthropomorphizations. It is the Light and the One, in manifestation.

Each of these triple numbers describes a complex formula as an analysis of the nature of the first nine number-qualities in Gothic lore. These and other numeric mysteries are likely deeply encoded into the text of the Gothic Bible.

## Gothic Gamatria

The symbolic numerical analysis of the mysteries of the Gothic Bible will have to wait for another time. All I can hope to do here is lay a groundwork for further study by a researcher with more qualifications and temperament for this field of work. Every objective fact points to the idea that such numerical and symbolic links were familiar to Ulfilas and to his contemporaries, Greek, Roman and Gothic.

The basic theory of gamatria is that since all letters are numbers, then all words are numerical formulas which can be added together to provide a sum which renders a higher numerical identity, just as a collection of phonetic signs strung together render a *word*, a semantic unit. The higher numeric sums of words, e.g. Gothic *hauhhairtei*, pride arrogance, *aurkjus*, pitcher and winja, meadow all add up to 521. This demonstrates that there is an esoteric affinity between these apparently disparate words. Therefore it can be said that a hidden affinity, or higher esoteric identity, exists between these two words, despite their apparent mundane semantic differences. The system of affinities can also be extended into the area of multiples of basic numbers. This whole network of hidden meanings in a linguistic text provides an alternate mode of esoteric interpretation of that text.

That such gamatria was both known to Ulfilas and that he intended it to be used as an esoteric key, is perhaps indicated by a comparison between the Greek and Gothic forms of the title "Christ." In Greek this is Χριστος (600.100.10.200.300.70.200 = 1480), while in Gothic it is 𐍇𐍂𐌹𐍃𐍄𐌿𐍃 (600.100.10.200.300.70.200 = 1480). That the number systems have been coded in such a way as to form an identity between the Greek and Gothic forms of this title constitutes an esoteric signature indicating the link between the two systems.

It can be seen that gamatria forms a higher, more abstract, type of poetry. Becasue of its abstraction, and because number forms all sound, it transcneds any *one* particular language in an esoteric sense. Hence, though number languages can be cross-coded, and cross-decoded. In this manner Gothic and Greek words, for example, can be esoterically linked. Here are some interesting examples drawn from Gothic and Greek vocabularies.

All adding up to 164 are Gothic *ragin* "advice" and Greek ερημια, "solitude" as well as νηνεμια "calm." This indicates the necessity of solitude and calm in order to arrive at good — or divine — advice or counsel.

Adding up to 221 are Gothic *rūna*, "mystery" and Greek σιγη, "silence." We can draw from this that the secrets or the mysteries of the kingdom of god will be revealed in silence or stillness.

Curiously Gothic *hugs* "mind," and Greek στερνον "heart," as well as Greek γοης, "sorcerer," add up to 281. In Germanic anthropology the seat of the mind is thought to be in the chest, or nest to the heart.

Both adding up to are 318 Gothic *himins*, "heaven" and Greek 'Ηλιος, "sun." Here clearly the link between heaven, the supernal abode of god, and the sun is reinforced.

The word for "king," *piudans* and Greek ρειθρον, "river" and οδος, "way" all have 344 as their sums. This esoterically shows that the king, kings such as Alaric and Theodoric, were actual rivers or ways to their peoples and were, in their very beings, indicators of the right path for the people to go, as well as being responsible for their sustenance. These were sacred kings.

The Greek phrase 'ο λογος, "the word," and the Gothic term *weihiþa*, "sanctity," both add up to 443. The word in question is an aionic word which comes to the earth from a supernal aion, a sanctified place, and which is uttered in order to alter the current course of the world's development.

Linked to this is the number 575 which is the sum of Gothic *waurd*, "word" and Greek ετος, "year," and the Greek phrase τις ειμι, "who am I?" The word in question is again the *logos*, which is a key concept which a magus must utter at certain critical aionic times, or "years." The esoteric answer to the question: "Who am I?" is "Thou art the Word."

Additional examples of such insight run into the hundreds when the body of numerical values of the Gothic and Greek vocabularies are cross referenced. The archive at Woodharrow contains a complete numeric analysis of the known Gothic vocabulary.

One of the most remarkable discoveries in the field of gematria in the Gothic tradition has to do with the number 616. As noted briefly before, there is an alternate tradition regarding the so-called number of the Beast mentioned in Revelation 13.18. This indicates that the number is 616, not 666. What is remarkable is that the name of the Gothic letter X *iggws*, which means Man, or god-man, and is used as the initial letter in the name Christ, has the numerical value of 616. This points to the esoteric identity between the Beast (who is referred to as "a Man") and the Christos (who also became *human*) in the final stage of the apocalypse— a coded reference to the doctrine of universal salvation.

The whole area of Gothic gamatria awaits a master-work to be created by someone who will be able to decode this great Gothic mystery.

Chapter Four

# The Hidden Treasures of the Goths

In ancient, pagan, times the Goths were accustomed to managing two separate and different treasures, or treasuries. One was the royal treasure, which was derived from monetary fines imposed by the king on the people for transgressions. This was a sort of "taxation." The second was the so-called old-treasure, which was an ever increasing amount derived from tribute paid by foreigners and from booty collected in military campaigns. The royal treasure was used for regular state or tribal expenses, the old-treasure was maintained as a talisman of the kingdom and a guarantor of its continuance and legitimacy. The old-treasure had a magical and holy function, which was not supposed to be tapped into unless the existence of the nation was in danger. Of course, the old-treasure was also the source for funds to be paid to the retinue of the king and to the Gothic nobles.

One of the most distinctive and enduring aspects of the mysteries of the Goths is their frequent involvement with hidden treasures. Often these seem to be metaphysical or symbolic, but more often still they entail actual gold or other valuables. It seems to have been a Gothic cultural trait, in part inherited from the Germanic past, to hide symbols both to transfer them magically into the future or into another realm of reality and to increase their power through this process of *hiding*. Sometimes of course, it also appears that the treasures were hidden in order to preserve them from hostile forces. Only later would they be rediscovered and thus be restored to a place of honor.

## The Treasure of Pietroassa

In 1837 two farmers from the village of Pietroassa in Walachia, present-day Romania, found a golden treasure hidden under a limestone block in the ruins of an ancient Roman fortress. The objects were gold, some of them decorated with semiprecious stones. At first these farmers hid the treasure at home. Then after a year they sold it to an Albanian stonemason, Athanasius Verussi. There were originally twenty-two pieces in the hoard, but only twelve seemed to have survived Verussi's ownership. There was a torque, a ring with runes, a flat bowl, a canister, a bowl bearing a frieze of figures, a necklace, one large fibula and three smaller ones, as well as two small basket-like vessels. These eventually found their way into a museum in Bucharest.

Among the items "lost" before the first transfer to the museum was another ring bearing a runic inscription.

In 1875 the items were stolen from the museum, but were rediscovered a few days later. The rune-ring had by that time been largely destroyed by a goldsmith, but luckily the inscription survived— even if what was left of the ring was broken in two, thereby damaging one of the runes. The treasure was stolen once more and rediscovered before being looted by the Russians in 1916 and taken to Moscow as the Romanian army retreated during the First World War. There the treasure remained, lost and ignored for forty years until it was returned to the National Museum in Bucharest in 1956. (Krause 1966, pp. 91-92)

It was widely thought that this treasure represented pagan religious relics and that here we are dealing with a pagan Gothic temple-treasure. However, it clearly seems that the treasure relates more specifically to the symbolism of Gothic royal authority. Of course, the concepts of "state" and "religion" would have been closely intertwined among the pagan Goths. One theory has it that the hoard was deposited by Athanaric as he and his army retreated before the Huns in 376 or 380. This is unlikely on two counts. First, the treasure was perfectly transportable and would not have impeded the mobility of an army. Second, some of the items in the hoard have since been more positively dated to sometime in the fifth century.

The fact that the treasure was deposited in a fortress — a stronghold of chieftains — and appears to have been concealed or hidden rather than *sacrificed* indicates that it was intended to be recovered later by those who deposited it. As it turns out, the treasure proved to be a message to the world to come.

We can know a good deal about this treasure as it was actually provided with a *voice*, i.e. the runic inscription which miraculously survived on the simply designed neck-ring. For the Goths and the Germanic peoples in general at this time, the symbol of royal authority was not a *crown*, but rather a neck-ring. In a magical sense this might seem to indicate that the importance of the throat and voice of the king as a cultic speaker.

An old drawing of the ring preserves for us the general shape and design of the object, shown in plate 4.1. This reveals that the runic inscriptions was carved to sit across the throat of the wearer. It is unclear as to whether the runes would have been visible to observers when the ring was being worn. I would guess that the inscription was made to be hidden, as an operative message to forge a sacred link between the king/chieftain and the gods and the people.

Plate 4.1: The Ring of Pietroassa

The runes on the inscriptions read:

**gutaniowihailag**
*Gutanī ō(þal) wīhailag*
"The Goths' ancestral property, sacrosanct"

This would mean that the first word *Gutanī* is a genitive (possessive) plural of the tribal name of the Goths, and that the seventh rune is an ideogram or *Begriffsrune*, where the single rune ᛟ stands for the rune-name *\*ōþala*, "ancestral property." The use of this particular rune as an ideogram for its name is also well known in Anglo-Saxon manuscript practices, where, for example, ᛟ is made to substitute for Old English *œþel*, "country, native land" in *Beowulf* and other works. Finally, the complex **wihailag** is most likely the composite of *wīh* and *hailag*, following the usual runological rule of not doubling runes. These are the two forms of the "holy" known to he ancient Germanic and Indo-European peoples. The Roman philosopher Cicero combined the equivalent terms in Latin *sacer* and *sanctum* into the compound *sacrosanctum*.

Evidence also shows that there was originally a swastika or triskelion inscribed on the ring about where the 7th and 8th runes are. This might have been an older symbol, which the runes made more explicit. Because ᛟ indicates ancestral property or even real-estate or homeland in a more abstract sense, it is not likely that the ᛟ in any way is intended to indicate the treasure itself. The runic symbol ᚠ indicates mobile property and even gold, so clearly there would have been a symbol to designate the treasure if that is what was intended.

91

Rather, I believe, the inscription refers to the king's (or other chieftain's) function of keeping the "homeland," i.e. the community of Goths *sacrosanct*, i.e. set apart as holy or consecrated and invulnerable to harm. This was the sacred duty and function of the king, and this ring, a symbol of his sovereign power, would have clearly been seen as a tool to aid him in the exercise of this essential function.

As a treasure this ancient Gothic message impresses upon us the necessity of group identity and solidarity in a hostile world and that the true leaders are responsible for providing for and leading us toward these noble ends, which, when preserved, ensure our continuity and security. Such treasures exceed all gold in value.

## The Visigothic Treasure of Alaric

This treasure, certainly the most famous and storied of all Gothic treasures, is also sometimes falsely called the "Temple Treasure." This misdirection is understandable from the point of view that Europeans, once they had been Christianized, began to focus their interest on aspects of Jewish myth and history and at the same time began to ignore their own indigenous traditions. The treasure in question is actually the *Roman Treasure*— the contents of the Imperial treasury of Rome. This treasure had been built up for centuries by the Romans, and was without doubt the greatest single collection of wealth in the world known at that time. When Alaric sacked the City of Rome in 410 CE it is explicitly stated that he removed the entire contents of the treasury and placed it in wagons— which some say make a train requiring a whole day to snake its way out of the city. The Visigoths left for the southern part of Italy. where Alaric died. It had been his plan to cross into northern Africa to establish a new Visigothic kingdom there. Of course, some portion of the treasure would have been buried with the king in the royal custom of the Germanic peoples. Although the Visigoths were nominally Arian Christians, the old, originally pagan, traditions continued unabated in the royal clans. This treasure has been the object of treasure hunters— although it is likely that the grave was looted in antiquity, since it would have been in an area subsequently unprotected by the Visigoths.

It is well-known that the Roman treasury at one point contained the contents of the Jewish temple in Jerusalem, taken by Titus from that city in 70 CE. some of it is even explicitly shown on the Arch of Titus in Rome, where for example the *menorah* — or seven-branched candlestick — can be clearly made out in the sculpted image on this arch of the Triumphal march celebrated in Rome for Titus after his subduing of the rebellious Israel.

Writing in *The Jewish Wars*, the Jewish historian Josephus relates:

> Most of the spoils that were carried were heaped up indiscriminately, but more prominent than all the rest were those captured in the Temple at Jerusalem-a golden table weighing several hundredweight, and a lampstand, similarly made of gold but differently constructed from those we normally use...After these was carried the Jewish Law, the last of the spoils...Vespasian made up his mind to build a temple of Peace...There too he laid up the golden vessels from the Temple of the Jews, for he prided himself on them; but their Law and the crimson curtains of the Inner Sanctuary he ordered to be deposited in the Palace for safe keeping. (Josephus, pp. 385-6)

This description cannot be substantiated. Vespasian was emperor when Israel was subdued by Titus and the was temple destroyed. Titus became emperor in 79 and ruled to his death in 81. The general Roman attitude toward the Jews and their religion was one of disdain. Writing in the first decade of the second century, the Roman historian Tacitus refers to the religious practices of the Jews as "sinister and revolting" (*Histories* V.5) and he showed no reverence or awe with regard to the temple of the Jews or its traditions. Given that the actual Roman attitude toward the Jewish religion was so negative and disdainful, it is most likely that eventually the sacred objects taken from that temple were melted down and used for other purposes by the Romans, long before the Visigoths arrived to transport the treasury away.

Also, speculation that the Roman treasury contained the Ark of the Covenant seems unfounded. The ark was likely looted from the temple in antiquity by the Egyptians, Babylonians or Greeks. It must be remembered that the temple treasure of Jerusalem, as magnificent as it might have been, would have been a modest one as compared to those of other more powerful neighboring countries, as Israel was in fact a small and relatively poor country.

Alaric's sacking of Rome was not a particularly violent act. The Visigoths simply took possession of the city and in an orderly fashion excised the Roman treasury. A certain amount of the wealth of this treasure would certainly have been immediately divided among the chieftains and princes of the Visigoths. It was the greatest virtue of a Germanic king to be the "ring-giver," i.e. distributor of wealth to his fellow nobles within the tribe and especially to his retainers. After Alaric's untimely death the bulk of the treasure would have eventually made its way with the Visigoths back northward from Italy into southern Gaul under the leadership of Athaulf sometime in 412. There the Goths formed a stable kingdom centered around the cities of Toulouse and Carcassonne. The greatest king in the history of this particular Gothic kingdom was Alaric II (484-507). This kingdom endured intact for nearly a century. It was greatly reduced in size after the defeat of Alaric's Visigoths by the Franks at the Battle of Vouillé. Wolfram notes that after the battle with the Franks nevertheless "the greater part of the Visigothic royal treasure was saved." (Wolfram, p. 243) But parts of the kingdom near the coast continued to carry on as a Visigothic realm into the 7th century.

During this long period of relative stability and localized settlement, the Visigoths must have dealt with the enormous wealth of the Roman treasury in various ways. The fact that the wealth was not used to pay tribute to potential enemies, in order to avoid conflict, the way the latter-day Romans had often used their wealth, speaks to the fact that the gold was not valued in the same way by the Goths as it was among the Romans. In Germanic tradition gold is seen as a potential cause of dissension among kinsmen and something which must be distributed and circulated within the tribe in order not to exercise a destructive influence. Alternatively, or perhaps additionally, such gold can be buried or hidden more or less permanently and secretly concealed in a hoard— apart from the world of men.

Archeologists have noted the great influx of gold that came into Scandinavia around the middle of the 400s. The source of this influx does not appear to be local mining. It must therefore have come into Scandinavia from the outside. The logical source for this would be the Visigothic reserves.

A certain portion of the treasure — that part of it not hidden away — would have been removed to the Ostrogothic capital of Ravenna when Theodoric the Great became king of the Visigoths by right of conquest after the battle of Catalonia around the year 512.

So when we consider the fate of the great Roman treasure, we see that it was largely redistributed over at least a hundred year period— largely melted down and refashioned into objects appealing to the tastes of the Germanic peoples. This includes, for example, the many bracteates formed in Scandinavia between 450 and 550 CE. The design of these was most often modeled on Roman coins. The Roman gold paid Visigothic leaders and their allies and over time seeped back into the usual repositories of such wealth. However, a good deal of the treasure must have also been hoarded within the territory of the Kingdom of Toulouse. Most likely this was in the city of Carcasonne, although some like to think it was deposited in the area of Rennes-le-Château. We will come back to this question in chapter 6.

For the ancient Germanic peoples such gold — or any symbol of wealth — had two proper or right functions: 1) circulation and 2) separation. It was to be circulated among the people for practical reasons— to pay the for services and to reward their loyalty (especially in battle). But because it was seen as something of an extraordinary nature— something ultimately derived from beings beyond the realm of *Midjungards* — a good part of it was to be "sacrificed," given over into the transcendental worlds whence it came. This is why it was often secretly buried and "forgotten"— transferred to a higher place.

Clearly the Germanic idea of a "golden treasure" exists on two levels— a historical/practical and a metaphysical/transcendent one. As with the mythic treasure of the Nibelungen — perhaps inspired by the historical Visigothic treasure — it can become a curse and obsession if *too much* of it is brought into mundane availability at once. The treasure may exude more value from a hidden realm than in a historical/ mundane one. What is truly valuable is the tradition and the idea of unlimited power *just beyond the reach* of mortal man.

In the next chapter we will discuss the role of the Visigothic treasure in the modern mystery of Rennes-le-Château.

## The Treasure of Fuente de Guarrazar

The Visigothic Kingdom in the west extended across the Pyrenees well into the Iberian peninsula, into what is today Spain. After the demise of the Kingdom of Toulouse it was in Iberia that the Goths maintained their main stronghold in the west. This became known as the Kingdom of Toledo, for it was there that they had their capital. Of course, some of the old treasure was at these kings disposal.

As we know, the Goths were later pushed back toward the Pyrenees with the Islamic conquest of most of Spain in 711 CE. In the Arabic chronicle of Al Kazradji it is reported that Tariq, the Muslim commander, found twenty-five gold crowns of the Gothic kings, crowns encrusted with jewels, when he took the city of Toledo. It was further reported that it was the custom for each of the kings to have his own crown, each bearing his name.

Of course, it was thought that these crowns would have been melted down by the Muslims, which they probably were. However, there were in fact a total of thirty-three kings of Toulouse and Toledo from Athaulf in 411 to Roderich (Rodrigo) in 711— spanning three hundred years of Gothic rule in the west...

The summer of 1858 was turbulent in central Spain— heat waves alternated with great downpours of rain. On the morning of the 25th of August a group of farmers set out from their homes in the village of Guadamur just outside Toledo to work in the fields. As they passed the area of the spring of Guarrazat at the head of the rivulet which feed the small river of Guarajaz they noticed that some of the large slabs of rock had been displaced by the floodwaters. The shift of one of them had revealed an open space below it. It was a chamber which had been sealed with "red cement," or Roman cement. When the farmers looked inside they could see the glints given off by golden objects encrusted with semiprecious stones. At first they kept their discovery secret. Later they came back under the cover of darkness to remove the objects.

These turned out to be seven large golden crowns inlayed with stones, fourteen smaller but similar crowns, a golden dove, various vessels, candlesticks, brooches, and spindles for wool, all of which weighed a total of over three hundred pounds.

About six months later the French journal *L'Illustration* reported in its February 1859 issue that the French government of Napoleon III had acquired a treasure which had belonged to the Visigothic kings of Toledo. How did this Spanish treasure get into the hands of the French?

It seems that the farmers sold the golden objects to two goldsmiths in Toledo. These goldsmiths melted down most of the objects other than the crowns. Through some work of espionage the French government learned of this treasure. One day a French artillery officer, whose name remains unknown, but who is known to have had ties to Achille Fould, the Minister of Culture under Napoleon III, presented himself at the goldsmiths' shop and bought the remaining objects. This officer then secretly crossed the Pyrenees into France with the priceless treasure into. The crowns were eventually displayed in the Cluny Museum in Paris.

One of the original farmers who found the treasure seems to have been more clever than the others. His name was Domingo de la Cruz. He secretly returned to the place where the treasure was found and looked around some more. He found another treasure chamber and removed the contents. This smaller treasure consisted of the magnificent crown of King Swinthila, several smaller crowns, a golden belt with jewels and several crosses. De la Cruz sold some of the pieces but hid most of the objects in flower pots. The Spanish government sent investigators to the region in 1861 to discover whether more treasure could be found there. The farmer was questioned by Don Antonio Flores, the Secretary of the Royal Government. The farmer was convinced it would be in his best interest to give up his treasure to the Queen, Isabella. De la Cruz received a reward of 40,000 reales and an annual stipend of 4,000 reales. Now at last the Spanish could display at least a part of the treasure of Fuente de Guarrazar on Spanish soil.

During the Second World War, the Spanish Fascist leader Francisco Franco petitioned Marshal Pétain, the leader of Vichy France, for the return of the crowns. Vichy France was the southern part of France which more or less willingly cooperated with the Nazi occupation of the northern part of the country. Pétain returned the crowns to Spain.

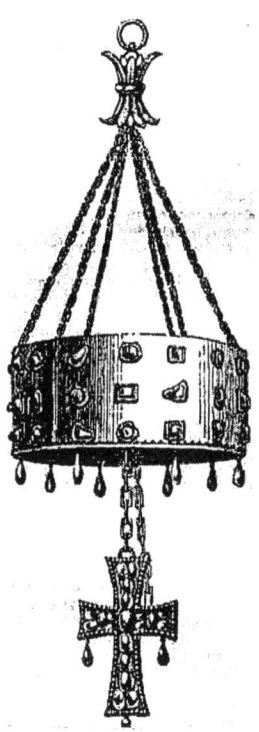

Plate 4.3: The Crown of Sonnica from Fuente de Guarrazar

The most interesting aspect of these crowns is the function they served. Originally they were displayed in the cathedral of Toledo. When a king was underwent his coronation he would then donate a crown to the church. Many of the crowns indicate by means of an inscription the king who donated it. Sometimes this inscription is in the from of bejeweled letters hanging on golden chains from the rim of the crown. A typical example of these inscriptions reads:

RECCESWINTHUS REX OFFERET
King Recceswinth offers (the crown).

Note the crown is not given to the king, but rather the inscription indicates that the crown is given (to the church?) by the king. The fact that the crown is meant to be *displayed* (hanging from golden chains) indicates that the object was probably valued more for its symbolic (spiritual) qualities rather than any monetary worth.

Since such practices of donating crowns by kings to be displayed in churches appears to be unknown elsewhere, we can only assume that this practice reflects an ancient and particularly Gothic belief of some kind. Semiotically the display of the king's crown in a church (or temple) is probably a hangover from the pagan times when the king's neck-ring might have been displayed on the altar of the temple. This is the probable function of the ring of Pietroassa. There it would be used in religious rites— and especially for the swearing of oaths. For the Visigothic kings, who are well documented to have still had pagan leanings, such a donation of a crown would have served his symbolic purposes, and the church would claim some benefit of prestige as well. The fact that an extraordinary attempt was made to save these symbolic objects from falling into the hands of the Muslims also speaks to their deep cultural meaning.

The treasure of Fuente de Guarrazar is more than gold. It consists of the idea of royal sovereign power and its inexorable linkage with the idea of the sacred. The fact that each king has his own crown and that he donated his crown in a repeated symbolic act as a part of a continuing sacrificial tradition speaks to the idea that the Gothic kings thought of themselves as sacral kings— not for any Christian reason, but rather because they had always considered themselves as such. The donation of the crowns reflects the mystery of the transmission of the royal sacrosanct power from one generation to the next. If anyone doubts the validity of the idea of symbolic values being passed over generations by the Goths, one only has to learn of the "Tower of Secrets."

## The Visigothic Treasure-Tower of Secrets

To this point the treasures discussed have all been a combination of gold and the symbolic qualities attached to the golden treasure. The Goths always seem to have had a high appreciation for the symbolic qualities of their treasures which exceeded the mundane value of them. Nowhere is this attitude more explicitly revealed than in the legend of the Visigothic Tower of Secrets.

Contemporary chronicles report that the Visigothic kings had for generations preserved a certain "House of Secrets," also referred to as a "Tower of Secrets," or the "Enchanted Tower." It was a structure in the old fortified city of Toledo with a chamber at its highest point guarded by a locked door. This door did not simply bear one lock, it was locked with a lock for each of the kings of the Visigoths throughout history. For it was the custom of the Visigothic Kings of the Kingdom of Toledo upon their coronation to go to this House of Secrets and instead of opening it, they would place yet another lock on its door.

When, in 710, the Visigothic King Witiza died, the Kingdom was divided in its loyalties. The Muslims were already dangerously advancing on the southern coasts of Spain. As was, and had always been, true Germanic custom, the council of elders was gathered to *elect* the new king.

Roderich (Spanish: Rodrigo) was elected. His qualifications included an aggressive bellicose nature, which seemed to be a necessity in the coming period of warfare. He underwent the royal coronation according to Visigothic custom. His crown now hangs with the many other crowns of the Visigothic kings in a museum in Toledo. But shortly thereafter he proved his aggressive nature would lead to disaster immediately when he went to the House of Secrets. Instead of providing the door with another lock, he broke the locks off the door and stepped into the chamber— unseen for centuries by the eyes of the kings. He opened what appeared to be a treasure chest in the center of the room— on it was written words which indicated that his kingdom would fall and that the reign of the Visigoths would come to an end in Spain. The document referred to images which came alive on the walls of the room— showing the invasion of the Muslims and the ultimate defeat of the Visigothic army.

Also among the treasures supposedly contained in the House of Secrets was the legendary "Table of Solomon," which was thought to be part of the loot from the Temple of Solomon in Jerusalem brought to Rome by Titus. As we have remarked, it is most likely that the greater portion of the items taken from Jerusalem were probably melted down by the Romans themselves. Other items my have survived in their original forms. Among these might have been the fabled "Table of Solomon."

Rodrigo's violation of the sacrosanct tower was a violation of the principle of the Mystery itself, which the ancient Goths would have known and preserved as *rūna*. This violation constituted the mythic act which brought an end to the reign of the Visigoths in Spain. The Mystery, which the *symbol* of the "Tower" represented, was to be *sought* not in violating the symbol but in *respecting* it, by adding another lock to protect her. Perhaps this tower was also a dim cultural remembrance of a myth similar to that of the Norse *Hlíðskjálfr*, the tower of Óðinn. Through the symbolic act of adding another lock, the true King demonstrates his understanding of the Mystery which dwells both within and without himself. With his Understanding the exercise of true sovereignty is possible, without it disaster will strike— whether it is in the life of a Nation or of an individual.

## Chapter Five
# Spears of Destiny

Among the splendid objects of the imperial regalia now housed in the Hofburg in the heart of Vienna, Austria is the by now infamous "spear of destiny." A good deal of myth, both ancient and modern, has built up around this object. The shear amount of mythology and its often sensationalistic character requires us to turn a more careful and sober eye to the actual history of the object in order to allow the more traditional mysteries surrounding it to reemerge once more. In ancient, pre-Christian, times a spear was the most typical weapon used in the Germanic world as a sort of royal scepter. It was a great symbol wielded by freemen in the Germanic world. In the assemblies men would often cast a "yea" vote by lifting their spears aloft and shaking them— hence the names Shakespeare (English) and Notker (German). A king's spear was not only a sign of his own status, but also one of the protection and solidarity of the folk he represented. As was the case with many another significant object or symbol from pre-Christian traditions, Christian apologists simply looked into biblical texts to discover a formal similarity upon which to create a "scriptural" basis for the continuation of the use of the symbol or object. It would have been fruitless for the apologists to demand the discontinuance of these usages, they simply had to re-sacralize them within Christian mythology. Then with enough passage of time the actual origins would be forgotten. In the early centuries of the Christianized Germanic world the spear remained an important symbol of royal power.

### Ancient Gothic Spears

Many centuries before the ancient Goths had heard of Jesus, the spear was of tremendous importance. We have already mentioned some of these objects in connection with the story of the syncretism between the Goths and north Iranian cultures, especially the Sarmatians and Alans (ch. 2). Here we wish to delve deeper into the actual meanings of these objects. Previously we noted that all of these spears, but especially those of Kovel and Dahmsdorf, show clear symbolic syncretism between the Germanic and north-Iranian worlds as they combine Germanic runic inscriptions (and linguistic forms which show them to be of East Germanic origin) with the typical "heraldic" devices of the

Sarmatians called *tamgas*. All of these spears were clearly ceremonial or ritual objects— not ones intended for actual physical combat. They are all more or less richly ornamented and show no signs of ever having been used in combat.

Now let us turn to a full description of each of these four spearheads:

The spear of Kovel (plate 5.1) was found by a farmer plowing his field in the village of Suszyczno near Kovel, Poland in 1858. It came into the possession of a private collector, Alexander Szumowski. After his death the spear vanished. In the fall of 1939, shortly after the German invasion of Poland, it mysteriously reappeared still in a special box created for it by Mr. Szumowski. Soon thereafter it was transported from Poland to Germany, where it again disappeared at the end of the war.

Plate 5.1: The Spearhead of Kovel

The iron object dates from around 250 CE. It is decorated wit silver inlay. These symbols appear to be both solar and lunar, coupled with a *tamga* and a runic inscription:

ᛉ ᛟ ᛁ ᛚ ᚨ ᚱ ᛁ ᛞ ᛏ
s  d  i  r  a  l  i  t

This reads from right to left: *tilarids*, which is clearly an East Germanic or Gothic form grammatically. This is the noun agent name of the spear itself, the literal meaning of which is something like "target-rider," or more generally, "attacker." (Krause 1966, pp. 77-80)

The spear of Dahmsdorf (plate 5.2) was discovered in 1865 during the construction of the train station at Dahmsdorf-Mücheberg near Lebus, Germany. The area contained a number of cremation graves, to one of which this object belonged.

This spearhead, like that of Kovel, dates from around 250 CE, and is made of iron with silver inlay. The decorations include solar and lunar signs, with a *tamga* and the runic inscription:

ᚱ ᚨ ᛉ ᛃ ᚷ
r  a  n  j  a

Again, reading from right to left, we have a noun-agent name of the spear *ran(n)ja*: "the runner," or "the one which causes (them) to flee." In the case of "the runner," it is meant in the sense of "to run someone, or something, through." This is also probably an East Germanic form, but the archeological and art-historical context make the Germanic origin of the piece more certain. Its location indicates that it might have belonged to a Burgundian.

Plate 5.2: The Spear of Dahmsdorf

The spear of Rozwadów was found in 1932 by workers in the suburb of this town. The find was in the archeological context of an East Germanic horseman's cremation grave. Again the object is made of iron with silver inlay. It was brought to the regional museum in Sambor. A drawing of the object appears on plate 5.3.

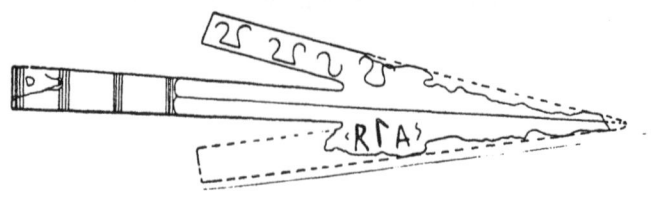

Plate 5.3: Spear of Rozwadów

The possibly fragmentary runic inscription appears to read: ḳrlus from left to right. The generally defies interpretation, although Krause boldly ventured *(i)k (e)ruls*, "I, the runemaster." The final *-s* form clearly shows this formula to be an East Germanic linguistic form. The other decorations may also be *tamgas*.

The spear of Moos was excavated from a cremation grave on the island of Gotland. It is now in the State Historical Museum in Stockholm. This spear is somewhat older than the others, dating from the as early as 200 CE. Its silver inlay work shows it belongs to the same general context of the other weapons considered here. The symbols on it cannot, however, unambiguously be identified as *tamgas*. It would not be surprising if the symbols were not *tamgas*, as Gotland would probably not have been in any way directly effected by Sarmatian interaction. No completely satisfactory explanation of the runic inscription has been established. It appears:

Plate 5.4: Spear of Moos

The runes can be read: ///gaois. This seems to be inscribed right to left *sioag-*, which makes no sense. Damage to the metal immediately to the left of the g-rune makes It unclear as to whether there was another character following (or in front of) the g. The reading **gaois** could be interpreted as Gothic *gaujis*, "the bellower." Krause says: "The name would then allude to the widely held belief in the ancient northern world, that a spear which emits a loud tone as the army marches into battle will bring its owner good luck and ruin to the enemy." (p. 81)

These spears are magical — highly symbolic — objects which acted as talismans in battle, as well as functioning as royal scepter— signs of the sovereign power of the king or chieftain. The spear, like other symbolic weapons, would become the focal point of the solidarity of the group— clan, tribe, or royal retinue. Without question such symbolic weapons would be handed down from generation to generation. Often such objects were buried for a time and then recovered by the family or heir to the previous owner. The object would thus gain in power for having been for a time in the other-world.

Most readers will not have to be reminded of the role of the spear as an attribute of the god Wōðanaz/Óðinn. He is depicted with a spear in northern art; the "Völuspá" (st. 24) has him inaugurating the "first battle in the world" by throwing his spear over the enemy army; he himself is said to be wounded by a spear (*geiri undaðr*) in his initiatory self-sacrifice by means of which he discovers the runes ("Hávamál" st. 138-139). Certainly, however, the spear is not entirely limited to being an attribute of Óðinn in the Germanic world. It can more generally be seen as the typical "royal scepter" of the Germanic king— which customarily bridges the first (sovereign) and second (warrior) functions.

## The "Holy Lance"

The "spear of destiny" is an object about which a good deal of nonsense has been written. This moniker was first given to the holy lance found in the imperial regalia in the Hofburg in an article in the *Sunday Dispatch* (Nov. 6, 1960) by Max Caulfield many years before the publication of Trevor Ravenscroft's scurrilous book on the subject. In general works on the lance range from understandable medieval re-mythologizing to modern obsessions with "occult Nazism." The purpose of what I write here is the bring to bear upon this mysterious object a factual and objective foundation of understanding, so that a truer sense of the original spiritual importance of the object can be grasped.

When the Germanic peoples were first Christianized their kings and chieftains typically carried spears as symbols of their sovereign power— a power ultimately derived from their own "divine blood." This divine blood stemmed from their god-like ancestors— called *anseis* by the Goths as we have seen. With Christianization apologists cast about in scripture to find a notable spear in biblical mythology, and found reference to the one used by the Roman soldier, identified in later Christian tradition as Longinus, to pierce the side of Jesus as he hung on the "cross."† Due to obscure passages in the Old Testament later interpreted as dealing with the signs of the true Messiah which imply "not a bone of him shall be broken" (John 19.36)†† it was essential in this mythology for Longinus to prove that Jesus was dead by thrusting the spear into him— otherwise his legs would have been broken to hasten his death so that the body could be taken down before the beginning of the Jewish Sabbath. It was therefore said that the spear of Longinus proved that Jesus was the Messiah, that at that moment Longinus held the destiny of the world in his hands and that subsequently he who possesses the spear similarly holds the destiny of the world in his hands. All this makes for a fine medieval Christian myth to syncretize the use of a spear by the kings with Christian symbolism— but it, like the "shroud of Turin," cannot have had anything to do with the life and death of the historical Jesus. The "spear of destiny" is a spear-blade of Germanic manufacture dating from the 8th to 10th centuries. In other words, it was forged some six hundred to eight hundred years after the death of the historical Jesus. Therefore all legends surrounding it before this time have no basis in fact. It could not have been connected with St. Maurice, Constantine the Great, or even Attila.

If the *sancta lancea* could not have belonged to a Roman soldier, what can we learn about its origins from its art-historical and other physical characteristics? It could have been forged among the Alamanni, Franks or Lanbgobards, as early as the 8th century, but no later than the 10th century— most probably it comes from around 800 CE.(Paulsen, p. 301) As a symbol, the spear clearly has its origins in pre-Christian usage. Albert Brachmann, writing in *Deutsches Archiv* 6 (1943), pp. 407-09, clearly outlines the development of the symbolism of the spear of Wodan into a spear of supposed Christian significance.

---

†Jesus is not described actually hanging on a cross in scripture. He is said to have drug a στυρος, "pole, stake," to his place of execution. This was actually a crossing beam for he arms which was then hoisted up onto a scaffolding. The use of a cross as a sign of Christianity only comes later in Europe due to syncretism with pagan symbolism.

†† One more of the countless fabrications found in Ravenscroft's *Spear of Destiny* (pp. xi-xii) says "Issiah had prophesied of the Messiah, 'A bone of Him shall not be broken.'" Issiah contains no such passage. The text is from the New Testament, John 19.36, which obscurely refers to Exodus 12.46, Numbers 9.12 and Psalms 34.20. Christian apologetics often deceptively use the techniques of either fabricating events on paper to fit prophesy or projecting tortured interpretations back onto murky passages to "prove" obscure theological points.

It appears most likely that the spear in question was of Langobardic manufacture. The transference of a spear is known to have taken place as a part of the Langobardic "coronation" ceremony for kings. According to Howard Adelson in his article "The Holy lance and the Heredity of the German Monarchy" [*The Art Bulletin* 48 (1966), pp. 177-191] this transference was more important than the actual reception of the crown by Langobardic rulers.

Through several centuries of the first millennium the Langobards, originally called Winnili, were geographically in close proximity to the East Germanic tribes as they migrated southward. The Winnili ("winners, strivers") migrated from Jutland to Pannonia (present-day Hungary) and then into the northern part of the Italian peninsula along the River Po around 558— after the official demise of the Ostrogoths in Italy. The Langobards then dominated northern Italy for the next two hundred years until they were defeated by the Franks of Charlemagne in 773-4. It is thought by some that Karl took a certain royal spearhead as a sign of his conquest of the Langobards and that it was this spearhead that became the *sancta lancea*. It is well-known that Charlemagne carried a spear, or even simply a spearhead, which functioned for him as a "talisman of royal power." It is said he never let it leave his possession, that he slept with it, it was the source of clairvoyant visions, and that when he fell from his horse one day shortly before his death the fact that the lance flew away from him some twenty feet was seen as an ill-omen. Despite their defeat by the Franks the Langobards continued to exert cultural dominance in northern Italy for centuries to come.

Another account of the *sancta lancea* says that a certain Langobardic Count Samson bequeathed such a symbolic spear to King Rudolf I of Burgundy (888-912), who subsequently lost it in battle to the German monarch Heinrich (Henry) I ("the Fowler"). It seems unlikely that the spear of Charlemagne and that of Heinrich I were one and the same object due to their variant origins. However, it is possible that both have symbolic origins as Langobardic royal scepters which had retained the Gotho-Germanic significance of being signs of royal power derived from an ancestral blood-line. The orthodox Christian myth would insist on the spear of Longinus being singular and unique, of course, while Germanic myth would encourage the existence of many spears of Wodan, or royal scepters. Although such men as Charlemagne or Heinrich would never have overtly identified themselves as being anything but Christians, nevertheless they also knew full-well that their independent power to rule was based on ancient, pre-Christian, ideas and customs. Their pagan customs and traditional beliefs were their only protection against becoming nothing more than dependent appendages of the Roman church. It was originally for this reason that symbols such as the royal spear were so important.

Eventually, the original pagan rationale behind the symbol was forgotten, For this pagan mythic basis to be lost entirely it had to be replaced by a Christian one. This underlying necessity for *ersatz* myths for established practices and customs or symbolic objects, times or places is the driving force behind the syncretizing of pagan and Christian traditions.

The deepest secret borne by the "spear of destiny" has nothing to do with the later superficial mythic overlay, but rather with the essential original meaning of the spear as a sign of the direct blood-line relationship between the gods and the tribal aristocracy who bore such spears as signs of their nobility, leadership and freedom.†

---

† The whole mythology expounded in the books *Holy Blood, Holy Grail*, and *The Da Vinci Code*, that Jesus did not die on the cross but escaped to the south of France where he sired a bloodline of "secret kings" is itself merely a syncretic Christianization of the Visigothic (as well as Frankish and all other Germanic) tribal traditions about the gods' engendering of noble bloodlines. The idea that Jesus was a "mere mortal" — if rather an *Übermensch* — fits well with the Gothic, Arian Christology. It is therefore most likely that if there is *any* merit to this tradition at all, that it was originally a Visigothic and Germanic one that was progressively Christianized over the centuries as its original message and purpose became lost to those who bore the tradition.

Chapter Six

# Notes toward the Esoteric Gothic Legacy

As Appendix C shows, the image of the Goths has great resonance through the centuries. Their histories and traditions taken up later and discontinuously by their spiritual inheritors is one thing, however, we wish in this study to concentrate entirely on the direct and continuous legacy of the Goths in the centuries immediately following their official "disappearance" from history. This study cannot hope to cover all of the possibilities of this largely esoteric process. Certainly the area of the world where this legacy hung on for some time was in the Pyrenees mountains and in the foothills of these mountains on both the French and Spanish sides of this particular mountain range.

Historically the Visigoths were pushed southward by the Franks from the early sixth century onward, and, of course, the Muslim conquest of much of Spain in the year 711 forced them northward into the same general region. Therefore the Goths geographically retreated into the mountains, but they also slowly faded into the surrounding populations, where their traditions were often heavily disguised as these were carried on in new forms.

On the one hand the Gothic traditions were absorbed into the local church culture — where for example we see the reflected in the famous pilgrimage route known as the "Way to Compostela" and its attendant lore and symbolism. On the other hand we also see how certain groups of Goths insinuated themselves among the local population, changing their obvious identities (or having them changed for them) while not losing their distinctiveness from the people around them. Curiously, these two apparently divergent directions — the church and the local subculture still found key ways to interact with one another productively.

## The Cagots

Up until the 18th century there were people living in southwestern France and northwestern Spain called the *cagots*. The word *cagot* [kagō] in modern French means "bigot" or "hypocrite." But it is clearly derived from what the dictionary calls "a party of outcasts in Béarn in the Middle Ages." On the surface the etymology of the word is unclear.

The Cagots lived in ways segregated from others. They lived in ghettos, could not enter the front of churches, could not be buried in the churchyard, received the Eucharist from the end of a long pole, could not intermarry with non-Cagots, and had to wear a special sign— a red patch on their shoulders in the shape of a hand.

It is often explained that the Cagots were tolerated in southern France, or in the province of Occitania, because this was a region which was accepting of alternate cultures — heretics, Jews, etc. — in the Middle Ages. The Cagots were identified as *"gavots,"* which is sometimes taken to mean "lepers," although every record shows them not to be leprous and in fact to be exceptionally healthy. They were described as being short, blond and most often having blue eyes. Religiously the Cagots were described as being pious, and one text recommends giving them alms "in thanks for their piety and separation." (De Séde 1980, p. 247)

The Cagots were first mentioned in writing in the late 1200s, by which time they had long been established in the region. The theory that they were actually the cultural remnants of the displaced Goths was first forwarded in 1625 by Oihenart who said that their separation stemmed from their foreign origin as well as their laxness in religious belief. One French dictionary, the 1935 edition of Quillet, forwards the etymology of the word *cagot* deriving it from the phrase *canis Gothi*: "dog of the Goths." The Occitanian dialect word for dog is *can* (← Lat. *canis*) rather than the standard French dialect form *chien*. Although the term *cagot* is used negatively in standard speech, the historical Goths are remembered honorably and positively among the peoples of far southern France, so if the etymological connection with *canis Gothi* is correct, the term was not originally one of insult. Rather it was possibly connected by analogy with a similar well-known medieval formula *domini canes*, "the lord's dogs," as a nickname of the Dominican Order. As such the terms would refer to the idea of dogs as "loyal servants."

The Cagots are seen as a group of people who were part of the Gothic migration into southern France after the Muslim invasion of Spain. There is even an Occitanian poem which reads in part:

> The land in which they were born
> Once upon a time was burned
> By a horde of Saracens,
> Whom God despised.
> Those who remained behind among us
> Are the last of an army
> Which could no longer advance.

In general it seems that their segregation amounted to a sort of *sacralization*. They were different, and maintained their status as a separate group. It also appears that the Cagots supported themselves and made themselves extremely useful by plying their trade as masons, stonecutters and carpenters. They were especially adept at constructing church structures— the very structures the main doors of which they could not enter. Cagots are said to have founded the town of Cauterets, to have built the Montaut-quarter in Toulouse, and the abby of Saint-Savin near Argelès. In general they built many churches in the region from the 8th through the 12th centuries.

It is widely believed that the Cagots became the chief architects for the Order of Knights Templar, and that when this order was brutally and criminally suppressed by the king of France and the pope, some Cagots went underground to form the *Campagnons du Devoir de Liberté* ("Companions of the Duty of Liberty"). This was a craftsmen's guild for the construction trades and is an important root of French Freemasonry. They, like other masons, indulged in the typical "twilight language" codes to conceal their real origins. They were said to be "sons of Solomon," and to have participated in the building of his temple, etc. Here again we have the usual transference of esoteric codes to more familiar or conventional forms in order to render them more *acceptable* to the conscious mind. The esoteric meaning behind this tradition is a reference to the supposed Gothic possession of the treasure of Jerusalem (of "Solomon"), which was brought to southern France by the Visigoths after it was taken from Rome in 410 CE. The basic grade system of the *Campagnons* betray a Gothic origin:

1. Fox
2. Wolf
3. Dog

The initial grade is that of the Fox— a wild, wily, yet still uncultured beast. This is the grade of the apprentice. The second degree is that of the Wolf— a highly socialized beast, hungry for the completion of the hunt. This is the grade of the fellow or journeyman who has to travel far and wide and has five years to complete his master-piece to become a Master of the company, or a Dog. The grade of Dog is that of the Master. It signifies someone who is fully attuned to higher things, to the tradition, and loyalty to that tradition— just as the dog is joyously loyal and obedient to its own higher master.

This tradition is closely tied to the esoteric origins of the practice of making pilgrimage along the famed Way to Compostela. Esotericists say that this pilgrimage route, initiated by the Visigothic abbot Witiza (750-821), is linked to the location (or former location) of the temple treasure of Jerusalem. This treasure, as we have seen, can definitely be traced from Jerualem to Rome and from Rome to southern France, where it "disappears." This "treasure" can also be interpreted to encompass all sorts of special powers and abilities which are hidden and handed down from generation to generation. In the case of the medieval Cagots, the ability to build buildings. This was not an old Gothic ability, but one that was acquired after the fall of the Visigothic Kingdom.

## The Visigoths and the Mystery of Rennes-le-Château

Several times during the course of this book we have mentioned the mystery surrounding the village of Rennes-le-Château in the Languedoc region of southern France. This is because 20th century legend has brought this village and events which took place there into the mythic sphere of the lost treasure of the Visigoths, or the "Temple Treasure." These events were also brought to bear on the generation of the modern legend reflected in the books *Holy Blood, Holy Grail* and *The Da Vinci Code.*

Succinctly put, the legend is this: Jesus of Nazareth was married to Mary Magdalene and did not die on the cross, but escaped to southern France where he sired a bloodline which was connected to the Merovingian Franks. This continuing bloodline represents the royal blood (the *sang real ~ san graal*) or "holy grail." What is more, this bloodline continues to this day, and has since the Middle Ages been persecuted by the established Roman Catholic Church as a heretical institution— thus forcing its secret continuance. This secret was rediscovered in the late 19th century by the priest of Rennes-le-Château, who became rather wealthy in gold either through, it is said, his discovery of the lost treasure of Jerusalem or though payoffs from the Roman Catholic Church to keep silent about his discovery of the bloodline of Jesus. (The truth is more mundane, as we shall see.)

One of the glaring shortcomings of this legend is that the Merovingians, as we have seen, formed the first alliance with the Roman Catholics. It was the Merovingians who initiated the centuries long alliance between the royal house of France and the Pope, an alliance which most famously persecuted and destroyed the Knights Templar. The modern legend, for its own good "reasons," as we shall see, misses the whole point that it is the Visigoths, the enemies of the Merovingians, who possessed a secret tradition about the power of a special blood line. Most of the secret traditions ascribed to the Franks, actually belong to the Goths. The Merovingians are known as those who betrayed Germania to Rome, and caused Germania to loose the advantage gained by the hard-won victory of the Goths. The Franks are the friends of Rome, the Goths are the eternal anti-Romans— at least as far as actual esoteric tradition is concerned.

Certain facts have been established about the "mystery" of Rennes-le-Château. These have been objectively researched and reported in the book *The Treasure of Rennes-le-Château: A Mystery Solved* by Bill Putnam and John Edward Wood.

There is no ancient evidence that the present site of Rennes-le-Château was named Rheddae in Roman times, or was later a stronghold of the Visigothic king Alaric II. The treasure of the Visigoths was preserved in the environs of the present day city of Carcassonne, not Rennes-le-Château.

The idea that the treasure was to be found somewhere around Rennes-le-Château was first concocted by the local parish priest, Bérenger Sauniere, who served there between 1885 and his death in 1917. This was apparently an elaborate hoax meant to disguise the fact that he was selling masses through the mail for a handsome profit. He used the money he got through this disapproved practice to renovate the church and its environs, as well as finance some of the luxuries of the life he enjoyed. The rumor was spread that he had discovered some of the gold belonging to the treasure of Jerusalem.

To this hoax another was added. A certain French eccentric named Pierre Plantard created the Priory of Sion (registered as a legal entity in May of 1957). Paper trails were fashioned which could be discovered in ways that showed that Plantard was a descendant of the Frankish king Dagobert II, one of the last Merovingians, and that the Merovingians were in fact the repository of the "royal blood" of Jesus. The "payoff" for this hoax, as far as Plantard was concerned, was that he could fancy himself a descendant of Jesus, and be the rightful and secret king of France.

Material from these two independent hoaxes were drawn together in the late 1960s, first by the French writer on esoteric topics, Gérard de Sède, and then by the British actor, television producer and writer, Henry Lincoln.

The 20th century hoaxes perpetrated by Bérenger Sauniere and Pierre Plantard and their willing accomplices actually had the effect of obfuscating the true myth of the lost treasure of the Visigoths— a treasure that was not only material but also spiritual. The myth is this: The treasure, a material and spiritual substance, was obtained by the Visigoths in the pursuit of an act of supreme symbolic power. This is proper to their esoteric and ancestral tradition. This treasure was distributed and circulated in order that it could live and be vital. Symbolic parts of the treasure were preserved in the area of the town of Carcassonne, the last stronghold of the Visigoths in southern France. Various esoteric traditions grew up around the spiritual qualities of the treasure. These were intended to convey special spiritual powers to those who discovered the secret. It had nothing to do with the bloodline of Jesus, but rather everything to do with the spiritual tribal ancestry of the Goths. To believe that the bloodline of Jesus is preserved in a certain family in France goes nowhere for the individual living in our world today— other than to imply, in a preposterous fashion, that we should acknowledge the patriarch of that family as the "king of France"(!) The Gothic secret, however, mandates that we should recognize the inner and secret sovereign kingship of ourselves. Knowledge of this secret, once truly understood can transform the life of any individual who perceives it.

# Appendix A
## The Pronunciation of Gothic

As we see in chapter three, Gothic was written in an alphabet probably invented by Bishop Uliflas for the purpose of translating the Bible. A more or less regular and consistent system of transliterating these letters into Roman letters was developed over the years by philologists. The question, however, remains as to how these words are to be pronounced correctly. The following is a general guide, although those who want greater details on this are referred to William H. Bennett's *An Introduction to the Gothic Language* (pp. 2-5) or Joseph Wright's *Grammar of the Gothic Language* (pp. 4-16).

The Gothic alphabet is transcribed as shown in table 3.3. Here we will discuss problems of pronunciation of those transcribed forms and their special combinations.

Of course, we have no recording of a native Gothic speaker. This system of pronunciation has been reconstructed by linguists based on comparative evidence within the Germanic family of languages, coupled with comparisons to Greek and Latin loan-words and representations of Gothic words and names as heard by Greek and Latin speakers, whose writing systems are more well-known as far as the sounds they represent are concerned.

### The Consonants

The letters *h, k, l. m. n, p, t. s, z* were pronounced as in modern English. *X*, used almost exclusively to spell the name/title *Xristus*, was pronounced as a [k].

The single letter *q* was pronounced as our modern combination qu- [kw-], so that *qens* was pronounced [kwens].

The *r* was lightly tongue-tip trilled [r], as in Spanish or southern German.

Both *b* and *d* had two values. After a vowel or diphthong (double vowel) these were pronounced as *fricatives*. The *b* in such positions was pronounced in a way similar to our *v*, but using both lips, not the top teeth and bottom lip. The *d* in such a position was pronounced as our modern English *th* as in fa*th*er. In all other positions the *b* and *d* were pronounced as *stops*, i.e. as our *b* and *d* in "birch" and "day" respectively.

The *f* can be pronounced as in modern English, however, it is likely that it, like the fricative *b*, was bilabial— performed with both lips, not the teeth and lip.

In most positions the *g* can credibly be pronounced as the hard *g* in "gift," however, it was actually also a fricative, which is properly performed by making the *ch* sound heard in German *ach*, while vibrating the vocal chords. When coming at the end of a word or before a final *s* or *t*, the vibration of the vocal chords was dropped. If *g* occurred before another *g* (*gg*) it represented the *ng* as in modern English "finger." This double *g* spelling follows Greek orthographic practice. If a *g* came before a *k*, the *g* also got an *ng* pronunciation, as in our word "ink," and this pattern extends to the combination *gq*, which would have sounded like our *nkw* in "inkwell."

The Gothic ʘ letter was pronounced as a combination of *h* and *w*, a perhaps more exaggerated variation of our orthographic representation of a similar sound *wh-*, as in "what." It is transcribed with the special character ƕ.

As in other Germanic languages, *j* was pronounced as in or modern consonantal *y*, as in "year."

The Gothic letter ψ, transcribed using the common Germanic thorn letter (þ), always represented a voiceless *th*, as in the word "thorn."

Although *w* usually represented the same sound as it does in modern English (i.e. the common Germanic *w*), when it occurred after long vowels, diphthongs, or consonants not followed by another vowel, e.g. in Go. *snáiws*, *waústw*, and *skandujan*, meaning "snow," "work," and "to overshadow" respectively, the *w* had the value of a short *u*. So these three words would be pronounced [snayus], [wostu] and [skaduyan] respectively.

## Vowels

The written Gothic vowel system consists of five simple letters *a, e, i, u. o* and four digraphs, or two-vowel combinations, *ei, iu, ai* and *au*. These latter combinations were not all diphthongs, but some represented simple vowels as well.

The *a* could be either long (as in "father") or short (as in modern German *Mann*). Vowel length was never marked in Gothic spelling.

Long *e* almost sounded like the modern English long *a*, as in "late." There was no short from of this spelling (the short *e* was written with the digraph *ai*).

Short *i*, as in English "bit," was written wit the single letter *i*, while the long *i* (pronounced "ee") was written with the digraph *ei*.

The *u* had both long and short versions, the long *u* was pronounced as the vowel in modern English "boot," the short version as the vowel in "put."

The written *o* (Ω) was always a long vowel, close to the vowel in English "goat." It was pronounced farther back in the mouth than the vowel in "go."

Etymologically, the spellings *au* and *ai* could represent three different sounds each. Modern scholars have often added diacritical marks to distinguish these, as in the following table:

116

| Spelling | Phonetic Values |
|---|---|
| au | aú = short o as in "not"<br>au = long ō as the "au" in English "aught"<br>áu = the diphthong "ou" in "house" |
| ai | aí = short e, as "a" in "hat"<br>ai = long open ā sound<br>ái = diphthong with the sound of modern English long ī as in "mine"). Modern German *ei*. |

There is some evidence that by the time of Ulfilas these sounds had fallen together so that *au* can conventionally be pronounced as the diphthong "au" and the *ai* as the diphthong in modern German *ei*.
To this we must add the diphthong *iu*, pronounced "ew."

In conclusion to this rough and ready description of the sounds of Gothic I append a phonetic transcription, using *English* indicators as seen in most modern dictionaries, of the Lord's Prayer found in chapter 2.

[At-ta unsar thu in himinam, wēhnī namō thēn. quimī thewðinassus thēns. werthi wilya thēns, swā in himina ya͟h ana erthī. hlif unsarana thana sintēnan gif uns himma daga. ya͟h aflāt uns thatē skoolans sīȳma, swaswā ja͟h wēs aflātam thīm skoolam unsarīm. ya͟h nee bringīs uns in frīstubnyī, ak lousē uns af thamma uvilēn; untay thēna ist thewðangarði ya͟h ma͟hts ja͟h wulthus in īwīns.]

# Appendix B
# History of the Word "Gothic" and its Connotations

The word "Gothic" is evocative. It is likely that many readers first picked up this book with no real understanding of the ancient Germanic tribes which belonged to the Gothic nation. Rather they thought of girls in whiteface make up and black dress with multiple facial piercings. The current connotations of "Gothic" run in the direction of fanciful medieval architecture or horror and vampire fiction. How did this happen? Is there a legitimate connection between and among the various connotations of the word "Goth" or "Gothic"? To answer these questions in context we will have to make a thorough study of the words "Goth" and "Gothic" through history.

The history of the word in antiquity is well discussed by Wolfram Herwig (1988, pp. 19-35). The name "Goths" first appears in Latin writings in the early first century CE. It first turns up as a reflection of a derivative weak noun, *Gutones*, which could mean either "the young Goths," or "the great Goths." A strong form, *Guti*, appears in writing around 150 CE. The former is used in the *Germania* of Tacitus, where the Gothones are located east of the lower Vistula river. The weak form with the -one suffix soon disappeared from the record, and only the strong form without the suffix persisted.

In pre-Christian antiquity the Goths connoted no more than one of the any Germanic "barbarians." The name did tend to replace the designation "Scythian" which had been used for peoples of the Russian steppe since the time of Herodotus. This first lent the Goths an aura of ferocity and cultural greatness, as the Scythians had been so considered by the Greeks. This "confusion" of the Goths with North Iranian peoples (Scythians, Sarmatians, Alans, Getae) was somewhat justified in that the Goths did to some extent meld with these peoples, however, the Gothic language, law and religion tended to dominate the symbiotic group.

For the most part during the ancient and medieval periods, the name Goth first denoted the Gothic people, an East Germanic tribal group. But beyond this it connoted two different things south and north of the Alps. To the south what was "Gothic" was fierce, warlike and destructive of civilization. Why? Because the Goths had defeated the Romans at Adrianople and killed the Emperor Valens, had sacked the Eternal City of Rome itself, had come to dominate the ancient Roman heartland under Theodoric, and had established their own non-Roman kingdoms in Italy, Gaul and Iberia. In short, the Goths were historical villains because they had overcome Rome in some symbolic sense. As Rome was symbolically identical with all things good and right—

regardless of whether pagan or Christian — the Goths must therefore represent the opposite. (This point psychologically indicates also the degree to which the Roman Catholic Church was merely another representation of *Romanitas*, or Roman imperial policy in a cultural sense.)

In the Middle Ages these opinions lingered, but Gothic prestige was also recognized in the south, most especially in Spain. The attitudes expressed at the 1434 ecclesiastical conference in Basel, where Spanish and Swedish delegates argued their countries' relative merits based on how "Gothic" they were, already demonstrates the persistence of this idea from antiquity.

With the Italian Renaissance, beginning in the 15th century, writers began to use the terms Goth and Gothic in increasingly negative ways. The Goth was the "anti-Roman," or anti-Classical symbol *par excellence*. Again proponents of Classical aesthetics made historical and cultural villains of the Goths. In the 1600s a "Goth" could mean a "rude, uncivilized, or ignorant person, one devoid of culture and taste." (*Oxford English Dictionary*) In this vein the particular "northern" style of medieval architecture which swept out of the north after around 1200 was also first called "Gothic" in the 1600s.

So in the 17th century we see that the term "Gothic," besides including the Germanic tribes of ancient history, also denoted 1) uncivilized, 2) Germanic in general, 3) medieval (non-classical), and 4) a style of architecture with pointed arches and tall pointed spires as well as a style of printed written character that looked like medieval letters.

Taking this into account, many political and social philosophers and reformers gravitated toward the new-found positive aspects of this set of ideas which were originally formulated to be largely pejorative. The Goth continued to be the quintessential anti-Roman symbol to Protestant thinkers of northern Europe who were critical of the Roman Catholic Church of the day. The Goth stood for the individual and liberty, the Roman for tyranny and absolutism. This historical-political symbology was more prominent in people's minds in the 1600–1700s than were the aesthetic labels.

In the late 1700s and early 1800s these ideas continued, but as the 19th century wore on, the Gothic revolutionary zeal was increasingly replaced by dark romantic longings. The Gothic became synonymous with the North. Northern Europeans, the English, Germans and Scandinavians, all to one degree or another identified themselves ancestrally with the Goths (even if this was only understood as a more Romantic term for "Germanic" in general). The Age of Romanticism idealized the "noble savage," so even if one accepted the (historically erroneous) idea that the Goths were violent savages, one could now all the more idealize them. They were our dark and half forgotten ancestors, they lived in a past age made dim with the mists of time, they were free and natural men, their sense of beauty was tinged with the sublime, and the Romantic sought to evoke this almost lost spirit.

Gothic literature, that category of literature comprising notions of Gothic romance and Gothic horror, can be said to begin with Horace Walpole's 1764 novel *The Castle of Otranto*, subtitled "a Gothic story." This style of literature only became in any sense popular in the 1790s with such "bestsellers" as Ann Radcliffe's *The Mysteries of Udolpho* (1794) and Matthew Gregory Lewis' *The Monk* (1796). Such literature is characterized by certain themes, settings, characters, aesthetic sense or philosophical viewpoints. The most typical set of circumstances in an archetypal Gothic novel include a strong-willed and intelligent young heroine who goes to live in an ancient palatial mansion in the remote countryside, where a powerful and mysterious nobleman resides, both enthralling and terrifying her. Prominent themes include a pervading atmosphere of darkness, the mysterious, and the supernatural, the presence of some ancestral hereditary sin or curse affecting the present. The atmosphere is charged with emotional extremes of passion and terror— both psychological and physical. The setting is most usually a gloomy and crumbling old house, or even a medieval castle or ruined monastery, and most often in a rural location. The remote locations evoked the heathen past, the outsider existence, beyond the bounds of civilization. The anti-Roman Gothic sentiment even found expression in the idea of the medieval Catholic Church being supported by cruel laws and exquisite tortures used to enforce that law, coupled with superstitious rituals. Gothic novels are populated with a series of often archetypal characters: a heroine who is often a governess or new bride, the brooding demonic and darkly handsome Byronic hero/villain, misfit servants, precocious children, and sometimes a mad relative in the attic or basement. Of course, the ghosts of dead ancestors also not seldom walk the halls. The aesthetic sense projected in these novels is one which emphasizes darkness and the inevitable decay of human creations. The sense of beauty is clearly that of the *sublime*— something which stimulates fascination and horror at the same time. Here the philosophy underlying the Gothic romance becomes more obvious. It is linked to the remote (ancient/ancestral) world, ruled by strong emotion, rejecting the "enlightened" smugness of the Age of Reason, and embracing the wild inner landscapes of nightmare and imagination.

The period of dominance for the Gothic aesthetic spanned the century between the 1790s and 1890s. However, the genre and all its thematic variations continued to find lively voices in the 20th century. Germanic Gothic influences were strongly felt in early horror films, especially those made in Germany and those produced in the United States at Universal Studios under the German immigrant Carl Laemmle.

The ideas of Gothic romance informed new generations of writers of novels as well. But more and more it was the horrific elements of the Gothic which resonated with the generation known as "monster kids" (those whose imaginations were formed between about 1950 and 1968). These went on to create dark visions which inspired yet a younger generation of neo-Romantics and "Goth girls."

In summary, the word "Gothic" went from describing an ancient Germanic tribe, to being a general designation for all such ancestral tribes, to becoming a metaphor for all things pertaining to the dim, mysterious past. It became synonymous with "a metaphysical North." One set of philosophical thinkers used this symbol to describe freedom-loving, individualistic Northman as opposed to the Roman who is content living under tyrannical slavery. On the other hand more artistic thinkers took this idea of the North and emphasized the emotional, inner (dark) world of the ancestral soul slumbering deeply within and awaiting rediscovery. In a sense there was a psychogeography at work— that which was Northern was dark, inward and remote — unconscious — while that which as Southern was bright, outward and present— conscious. The Romantic Gothicists embraced the inner world of their souls and its dark imaginings.

# Appendix C
# The Spiritual Heritage of the Goths
By Bishop **X**, GCG

The ancient ways of the Goths provide for us an esoteric context for understanding an essential part of our own heritage. The nature of these ancient traditions should be reviewed and focused upon if the message of Edred's present work is to be understood for what it is, or can be. In this work we see both the principle of development and tradition. That is, there is *development* over time, which allows for adaptation to existing and changing conditions, and there is the *essence* of tradition which hones in on the eternal values which are transmitted over time. At present the Gothic heritage is at a low point in its long history. Forgotten more than ever among the peoples in the traditional lands of the final Gothic stands — southern France and northern Spain — the heritage awaits a new awakening.

To describe the essence of the Gothic heritage, we must look at certain essential elements: the *anseis, stabeis*, the nature of God, the nature of the world, the nature of man as well as the institutions in the present world which are prepared to receive and carry on this heritage. Despite the hundreds of details which might be chalked up to the Gothic spirit, these are the elements which are essential, which we cannot live without in the Gothic realms.

The *anseis* are the ancestral gods. They are embodiments of the divine and they are encoded in the flesh of their descendants, as alluded to in Edred's seminal article "The Gothick God of Darkness." (There I feel sure that he meant "darkness" as a symbol of the *inner* world, not really anything "sinister.") The *anseis* are divine in that they are immortal and greater in being and consciousness than mortal and ignorant men. Yet they dwell not only above us, but also within us. The *anseis* are our spiritual selves. They can become incarnate in the world and carry out special missions. Each Goth carries within himself a divine nature, that of the *anseis*— a nature of which he remains more or less ignorant until he undertakes heroic-spiritual work.

The *stabeis* — the elemental letters of the Gothic alphabet — are seen as a roadmap to the world and self. They are the objects of study undertaken by the individual in order to become more aware of the divine-heroic nature slumbering within. The letters are specific and particular *Gothic* expressions of the secrets or mysteries expressed in the ancestral runes. In order to gain the deepest possible understanding of letters, they must be meditated upon both in their own right and to some extent in connection with the older runes and the Greek letters. (However, it would be a mistake to try to understand the *stabeis* entirely in terms of the runes— the *stabeis* are culturally universal signs.)

In the Gothic tradition the nature of God is grasped in the following way. God is the good (*þiuþ*). God is the One— in it is everything and nothing. God is the Father (origin) of all. God is light. His absolute godhead is transcendent, immortal and unchanging. That is, it is an absolute state of independence, permanence and perfection. From its fortress the Father engendered a first Son, who created everything that is good in the world and he used in his construction the plan inherent in the Holy Spirit— the eternal framework of being. This is the triad of the divine, the Father-Son and Holy Spirit. The Son gave rise to an innumerable — but not infinite — number of spirits who are the *anseis*.

The Son also gave rise to the world through an act of self-sacrifice before time began. The crucifixion and resurrection of the Son was a cosmic event before it was ever a "historical" one. This Son has become an incarnate being at various times in the past, present and will so again in times to come as humanity Needs him and his Message.

The Gothic tradition says this about the nature of the world in which we live: Humanity lives in the midst of the world. This middle-position — *midjungards* — is not related to physical space, but rather to abstract and moral being. There is a realm which is superior to the middle and one that is inferior to it.

The character of mankind is seen thusly in the Gothic tradition: Each individual is endowed with a divine spark, this is the *ansus* within. The individual is also endowed with the freedom to chose good or evil at every moment of life. We know that our homeland is above, with God, but the Evil One and its minions often fool us into believing it is below, in destruction. Every individual is destined to return to his divinity. In order to learn or our true natures it is necessary to have Teachers, leading-men or heroes, who show us the way.

Part of the past of our tradition is the subject of Edred's present book. I would be remiss if I did not at least mention the institutions which carry forth the Gothic tradition in its present form in the world today. These institutions have in the recent past been virtually secret, truly esoteric bodies. Some are members of them who are as yet unaware of their places in these bodies. It is hoped that this book will awaken their spirits. One such institution is the Gothic Church of God. It has twenty-seven living bishops around the world, many of whom remain hidden and unknown. If the contents of this book have awakened you to the knowledge that you may be one of these, write to the publisher of this book for further direction.

The structure of the GCG is made up on twenty-seven bishops and any number of parish priests with independent congregations. Priests are ordained by bishops. The teachings of the church can to some extent be gleaned from this book, and most especially from this appendix. But some of it remains secret.

This book has shown the secret of the Goths to be evidenced in their persistent identity and solidarity in the face of adversity and hostility in the world— history awaits a new generation of Gothic heroes to make manifest once more this ancestral spiritual heritage.

𐌲𐌰𐌿𐌰𐌺𐌽𐌹𐍃 𐌽𐌿

# Appendix D
# The Gothic Mission Today

Today in the western world we find ourselves in a state of decay, of anomie and confusion. We have lost our own authentic ways and are thus threatened all around and from within by hostile forces. The situation we find ourselves in is not unlike that of the collapsing Roman Empire. Some Fundamentalist Christian sects like to point to this fact as a "sign" that their historicized, and "dumbed-down," Apocalypse is neigh. Their sci-fi vision is the least likely. More likely is a repeat of what happened at the collapse of the actual Roman Empire. We have seen how an authentic tribal group, the Goths, were then able to pick up the broken pieces of the Empire and forge a new world from a synthesis of what remained and their own authentic elements. This process was one deeply imbued with the idea of Mystery — of *Rûna* — which led to new discoveries and which in turn was expressed in the well-known and much documented *heroic action* of the Goths.

How does Mystery lead to Action?

This is the new mission of the Goths in the present world.

The mysteries of the Goths raise more questions than answers. As such they are true mysteries, not merely conventional secrets. A true mystery inspires the subject, and thereby informs the subject in subtle ways which transcend mere factual information. A mystery is a mode of inspiring subjective, inner, excitement which fuels a quest for discovery.

Such a quest, undertaken rightly, inevitably leads to the discovery of many objective facts and realities. New lands are discovered and conquered during the ensuing migrations. Thus was the spirit of the ancient Goths. It is this spirit which today moves those inspired by the Goths of old to undertake their own mysterious voyages of discovery and great migrations of the soul. By delving into the specifically Gothic image and lore in history the voyager will discover the Germanic system of values.

Once this discovery is made a mysterious force moves the subject to action. The first sort of action required is inner. It requires the subject to come to a deep conviction of the rightness and genuineness of his feelings. This inner conviction is nurtured and facilitated by an infinite number of objective facts discovered along the way, but it takes on a life of its own deep within the soul. Such a conviction becomes the unshakable foundation of the person's being. This inner life is at the root of what appears to be a Gothic cultural obsession. Nothing else quite explains the centuries of utter fascination of western culture with the shadowy image of the Goths. From this inner foundation — and only from this inner foundation — effective outward action becomes possible. The historical Goths were a people of action— they did things. They moved across vast expanses, they fought in wars, they transformed religions and empires. But their secret, their mystery, lies in the idea that this action was motivated by an eternal source of life.

The mission of the Goths in the world today is the same as it was then. To follow the Gothic way is to seek the mysterious, be inspired to discover the unknown. Beyond this, however, the Gothic spirit calls upon us to act heroically on what it is we actually discover and to act in full awareness that one is remanifesting out of the shadows what is real and eternally valid and vital.

·SϘΚΕΙ·ΨϘS·ΚΠΝϘS·

# Select Bibliography

Baigent, Michael, Richard Leigh, and Henry Lincoln. *Holy Blood, Holy Grail.* New York: Dell, 1982.
Bennett, William H. *An Introduction to the Gothic Langage.* New York: Modern Language Association of America, 1980.
Burns, Thomas. *A History of the Ostrogoths.* Bloomington: University of Indiana Press, 1984.
Flowers, Stephen E. "The Secret of the Gothick God of Darkness." In *Blue Rûna.* Smithville: Rûna-Raven, 2001, pp. 37-44.
——————. *The Rune Poems* Smithville: Rûna-Raven, 2002, vol. I.
Gamber, Klaus. *Die Liturgie der Goten und der Armenier.* Regensburg: Kommissionsverlag Friedrich Pustet, 1988.
Gregory of Tours. *The History of the Franks.* Trans. L. Thorpe. Harmondsworth: Penguin, 1974
Haymes, Edward R. and Susann T. Samples. *Heroic Legends of the North: An Introduction to the Nibelung and Dietrich Cycles.* New York: Garland, 1996.
Heather, Peter. *The Goths.* Oxford: Blackwell, 1998, 2nd ed.
Heather, Peter and John Matthews. *The Goths in the Fourth Century.* Liverpool: Liverpool University Press, 1991.
Helm, Karl. *Altgermanische Religionsgeschichte. vol. II. Die Nachrömische Zeit. Pt. I Die Ostgermanen.* Heidelberg: Winter, 1937.
Ibn Fadlan. *The Travel Report of Ibn Fadlan as it Concerns the Scandinavian Rûs.* With Commentary by Stephen E. Flowers. Smithville: Rûna-Raven, 1998.
James, Edward. *The Franks.* Oxford: Blackwell, 1988.
Maenchen-Helfen, Otto J. *The World of the Huns: Studies in their History and Culture.* Berkeley: University of California Press, 1973.
Mierow, Charles C., ed. *The Gothic History of Jordanes.* New York: Barnes & Noble, 1960.
Josephus. *The Jewish War.* Trans. G.A. Williamson. New York: Dorset, 1959.
Karlsson, Thomas. *The Adulruna and the Gothic Cabbala.* [unpublished manuscript], [2006].
Krause, Wolfgang. *Handbuch des Gotischen.* Munich: Beck, 1968.
Krause, Wolfgang and Herbert Jankuhn. *Die Runeninschriften im älteren Futhark.* Göttingen: Vandenhoek & Ruprecht, 1966.
Paulsen, Peter. "Flügellanzen: Zum archälogischen Horizont der Wiener 'sancta lancea.'" *Frühmittelalterlichen Studien* 3 (1969), pp. 289-312.

Pennick, Nigel. *The Inner Mysteries of the Goths*. Freshfields: Capall Bann, 1995.

Putnam, Bill and John Edwin Wood. *The Treasure of Rennes-le-Château: A Mystery Solved*. Thrup: Sutton, 2005, 2nd ed.

Rice, Tamara Talbot. *The Scythians*. London: Thames and Hudson, 1957

Salti, Stefania and Renata Venturini. *The Life of Theodoric*. Ravenna: Edizioni Sear, 1999.

Schneider, Karl. *Die germanischen Runennamen*. Meisenheim: Anton Hain, 1956.

Sède, Gérard de. *Das Geheimnis der Goten* [= *Le mystère gothique*]. Freiburg/Breisgau: Walter, 1980.

——————. *The Accursed Treasure of Rennes-le-Château*. Trans. Bill Kersey. Worcester Park: DEK Publishing, 2001.

Streitberg, Wilhelm. *Die gotische Bibel*. Heidelberg: Winter, 1919-1928, 2 vols.

Tacitus. *The Agricola and Germania*. Trans. H. Mattingly. Harmondsworth: Penguin, 1970.

——————. *The Histories*. Trans. K. Wellesley. Harmondsworth: Penguin, 1975.

Thompson, E. A. *The Goths in Spain*. Oxford: Clarendon Press, 1969.

Thorsson, Edred. *Runelore*. York Beach: Weiser, 1987.

——————. *Green Rûna*. Smithville: Rûna-Raven, 1996, 2nd ed.

Vries, Jan de. *Altgermanische Religionsgeschichte*. Berlin: de Gruyter, 1956-57, 2 vols.

Wolfram, Herwig. *History of the Goths*. Berkeley: University of California Press, 1988.

Wright, Joseph. *Grammar of the Gothic Lanugage*. Oxford: Clarendon Press, 1954, 2nd ed.

www.ingramcontent.com/pod-product-compliance
Ingram Content Group UK Ltd.
Pitfield, Milton Keynes, MK11 3LW, UK
UKHW041947230426
12048UKWH00008B/193